GRACE AND GIGABYTES

GRACE
····· AND ·····
GIGABYTES
·············
BEING CHURCH IN A TECH-SHAPED CULTURE
·············

RYAN M. PANZER

Fortress Press

Minneapolis

GRACE AND GIGABYTES
Being Church in a Tech-Shaped Culture

Scripture quotations are from the New Revised Standard Version Bible © 1989 Division of Christian Education of the National Council of the Churches of Christ in the United States of America. Used by permission.

Cover Image: Ico Maker/Shutterstock
Cover Design: Brad Norr Design

Print ISBN: 978-1-5064-6413-8
Ebook ISBN: 978-1-5064-6414-5

To my daughter, Alice.
May your life be filled with grace, love,
and the joy of asking questions.

Contents

Preface

As I was preparing to graduate from Luther Seminary, I completed a course on digitally integrated ministry, the act of integrating pastoral care, preaching, and spiritual practice with new technology. Taught by Mary Hess, a professor of Christian education and leadership, the course began not with an extensive exposition of new tools or apps for ministry, but rather with a deep investigation into the culture of the digital age. What does it mean to preach the Gospel in a virtually connected community? What are the implications of pastoral care in a time of context collapse? How is faith initiated, nurtured, and developed outside of institutional church? In Professor Hess's class, I learned that culture precedes technology, that no ministry can be "digitally integrated" without a clear understanding of how digital technology shapes culture.

I have often heard church leaders, clergy in particular, talk about a need for "digital transformation." When I ask them what transformation looks like, they typically refer to something visible, like a website or a social media page. They rarely say anything about culture and the leadership transformations necessary for effective ministry in digital culture. I wrote this book to help those concerned with the future viability and sustainability of the Christian tradition learn how to approach the necessary work of transformation by first focusing on culture. If leaders want the church to do more than just survive in digital culture, they must set aside the focus on technological tactics and consider instead how technology changes the way we think, learn, and connect. When church leaders begin the conversation on digital transformation with the technologies themselves, they are merely flinging high-tech messages to a message-inundated society. Leaders may be using these platforms for marketing, but they're not using them for ministry.

This book is based on dozens of interviews with lay and ordained Christian innovators, those who understand that the ministries of this digital age need cultural transformation, not flashy digital tactics. It should come as good news that digital-age ministries do not require significant digital expertise. These ministries are an eclectic blend of high-tech, low-tech, and no-tech, online and offline, virtual and in-person. They do not share an expert-level approach to technology. They do share a commitment to embracing questions, deepening connections, facilitating collaboration, and fostering creativity. Accordingly, this book's chapters are based on conversations I had with pastors, lay leaders, and Christian educators who understand that ministry within digital culture demands a different way of doing church. As I was writing this book, I sat down with those who understand what it means to minister, and not just to market—to accompany, and not just to advertise.

I could not have completed this project without simultaneously living in the world of the church and the world of technology. Thank you to my world-class coworkers at both Google and Zendesk, two innovative and rapidly transforming companies where you can always bring your whole self to work. Thank you to the supportive community at Luther Seminary, especially the faculty and "Cohort 9" of the distributed learning program, both of whom helped me to discern what church transformation looks like in a world of many cultures. Thank you to the church innovators who agreed to share their stories and contribute their perspectives to this book, including Keith Anderson, Kyle Oliver, Sarah Stonesifer Boylan, Shamika Goddard, Kristin Wiersma, Heidi Campbell,

Mary Hess, Dave Daubert, Elizabeth Drescher, Jim Keat, Jon Anderson, DJ Soto, Jim Boyce, Darleen Pryds, Adam White, Joe Brousius, Stephanie Williams O'Brien, Eric Holmer, Sarah Iverson, and Jimmy Bero.

A special note of gratitude to my late mentor and friend Brent Christianson. Pastor Brent taught countless college students what it means to live a life of discipleship, inspiring us to lead, serve, and live faithfully. He taught me the joy of thinking theologically over cheese curds and pints of Lake Louie Warped Speed Scotch Ale. Because of Pastor Brent's mentorship and encouragement, I became a leader in the church, I attended seminary, and I wrote this book. I am eternally grateful for his friendship.

Thank you to those who helped me to recognize the importance of a life of reading and writing, especially my high school English teacher, Ann DeBruin. Though you left us far too young, your constant coaching made me who I am as a writer, while virtually eliminating the passive voice from my work!

Thank you to my lifelong friends who gather each summer at Rock Island State Park for three days of camping, cold beverages, and campfire conversations around life's biggest questions: Jim, Lars, Brent, Clete, Luke, Chris, and Martin.

Thank you to all who first brought me to church and introduced me to a God of grace, compassion, and transformation: my parents, Mike and Elizabeth Panzer; my siblings, Sam and Mari; and my beloved grandparents Joan and Tom Ryan.

I could not have even started this project were it not for the constant, loving support of my wife, Annie Wilcox Panzer. Better known as "Ms. Wilcox" to her high school science students, her constant support and encouragement kept me focused and continually reminded me of the joy of writing. As I was finishing this book, Annie and I welcomed our first child, Alice Catherine, into the world. Thanks to the two of you for the love and smiles that always keep me moving forward.

Introduction

If you have a smartphone nearby, pick it up. Open one of the apps that you regularly utilize and ask yourself what you use it for. Perhaps it's an application that allows you to take, edit, and share photographs with your community. Maybe it's a business tool that helps you to stay in contact with your customers and answer their questions. Open it and reflect on why you find it valuable.

In all likelihood, the app you just opened connects you with like-minded individuals. It's probable that the app facilitates collaboration so you and your connections can work together towards the achievement of a goal. It's also possible that the app allows you and your network to create something new, and to ask questions along the way.

There's something distinctive about each of the applications installed on that pocket-sized computer known as your phone. But what they all have in common is a design that facilitates questions, connections, collaborations, and creativity. You won't find an app on your phone that doesn't promote at least one of these. Most likely, your favorite app will facilitate all four. While many of these apps are powerful tools, those that are most useful to you represent a set of values found within our tech-shaped culture, a culture that—knowingly or unknowingly—you are a part of.

From nouns to verbs

I have spent my career within the seemingly divergent worlds of technology and the church, learning that in this tech-shaped culture, the two have more to do with each other than one might realize. Throughout this book, I'll tell stories and share perspectives from this intersection of church and tech.

I started thinking about this intersection as I began my career at Google. Though I wore many hats while working at the search giant, including the multi-color propeller hat given to "Nooglers" on their first day on the job, one of my main tasks was to call advertisers and offer them guidance on achieving their marketing goals. There's a reason the company creates jobs like the one I held. Google recognizes that successful advertisers turn into spendy advertisers, willing to fill Google's immense digital properties with a ceaseless reel of online promotions—and to line Google's corporate coffers in the process. As I spoke with a diverse base of customers—ranging from tree trimmers in Tampa to lawyers in Topeka to digital ad agencies in Toronto—I took note of the language used to describe how they and their customers experienced the internet.

Rarely, if ever, did they talk about users "going online." Never did they talk about users "looking" for their business. The words they used revealed something to me of the cultural behemoth my employer, and the technology it creates, had become. Advertisers described customer's interaction with the internet as "going to Google." They described the act of searching the web as "Googling it." Such language may well be familiar to you. Looking for movie showtimes tonight? You can Google it. Need the latest bus schedule? Go to Google Maps. And Google it. Asking me for directions downtown? Let me Google that for you.

Contrast the way we use Google as a verb with the word usage of an earlier time. Prior to our digital age, consumers would refer to a generic version of a product not with that product's description, but with the name of that product's most widely known brand. I could ask you to recall the most recent time you needed a facial tissue. But it would be easier for both of us if I asked when you recently needed a Kleenex. (Kleenex—that most analog of technologies—is a leading export of my hometown, Appleton, WI.) If I were in the southern United States, I could ask you for a soda, or pop, but it would be more efficient if I asked you for a Coke. These household brands illustrate a time when popular consumer products entered our cultural lexicon as nouns. Kleenex is something usable. During allergy season, it's often necessary. Coca-Cola is something drinkable; during a hot summer afternoon, it provides refreshment and a sugary jolt of caffeine. But as products invented before the digital age, Kleenex and Coke are objects for our use, products for our consumption. We refer to them merely as common nouns.

Now, in our tech-shaped culture—a time of networked connectivity, exponentially expansive computing power, and constant on-screen communication—we still refer to some products using nouns. "Microsoft Word" isn't used as a synonym for writing. "Kindle" isn't yet a stand-in for reading.

But in day-to-day conversation, the most ubiquitous and widespread technologies appear as verbs. Google—a juggernaut of search technology—is one such word. And it is, in fact, a word—at least according to the standards of the Merriam-Webster Dictionary.[1] As a verb, "Google" or "googling" defines the particular act of seeking specific information on the popular search engine. As the company's applications and platforms have become increasingly embedded in our online experience, the verb "to google" has expanded in scope, coming to describe nearly all acts of online exploration, perhaps even internet usage itself. Technologies of the digital era function as verbs because they are not products to be consumed, but platforms for participation in culture. We use words like Google not to describe things we all use, but to describe actions we all do.

Formed in 1996 by future Stanford dropouts Larry Page and Sergey Brin, Google started as one search engine among many long-forgotten competitors. As its market share increased, the company began expanding, providing an expansive arsenal of tools for social connectedness. Google started building messaging applications, launching Gmail as a beta product in 2004. They tapped into storytelling, acquiring YouTube in 2006, and then into collaboration, design, and storage—amalgamating many tools into Google Drive in 2012. Through it all, Google has been keenly attuned to the web's shift from desktop computing toward mobile connection. Their open-source Android operating system, launched in 2008, now powers over half of the world's smartphones, effectively guaranteeing constant user access to Google's ever-growing suite of products.

Since 2004, the company has been a disruptive force. Google has quietly acted as a co-conspirator in the killing of address books, Rolodexes, and daily planners. A competitor to Amazon's cloud storage business, the company continues to eliminate the need to store content on now-archaic relics such as floppy discs, CDs, jump drives—and hard drives themselves. Their pace of change, disruption, and innovation is startling, which may explain why so many of us are hooked. Every second of every day sees up to seventy-five thousand queries on the Google search engine. It is unsurprising that such a revolutionary player in digital technology generated nearly forty billion dollars in revenue over 2018, enough for third place in *Fortune's* ranking of the world's most valuable companies.[2]

Google isn't the only digital-age brand that functions as both a noun and a verb. These days, employees go to the office and "Slack" one another project updates, meeting requests, and stories from the weekend. Friends living in different cities record silly pet tricks and "Snap" them to their contacts. Coworkers no longer schedule a call—they

"Zoom" each other. And if web users have thoughts to share, those thoughts aren't written—they are "Tweeted."

Even amid increasing scrutiny over the industry's handling of user data and infringement on antitrust laws, digital technology continues to be a culturally transformative force. These technologies change not just our use of the web but our ability to apply information and knowledge to myriad situations and scenarios. "Google" has come to represent a new cultural process for searching and knowledge acquisition, for questioning, connection, collaboration, and creation. Google's peers have leapt from nouns to verbs because they transform culture and the way we construct meaning. They facilitate a new way of being ourselves, of being with one another, and of being with God.

From tools to values

Broadly speaking, we are living in a digital age. But to characterize the transformations of this period as a "digital age" is to understate the magnitude of disruptions since the normalization of connective and collaborative online technology. This is a time of upheaval, of profound cultural reorientation. Digital technology should not just be understood as it is often defined: as tools for the accomplishment of tasks. Major digital technologies—Google, Facebook, YouTube, Twitter, Salesforce, and many others—are better understood as a culturally transformative force. Together, they are pushing culture in a new, decisive direction fueled by four convergent tailwinds:

- These technologies nudge us to learn by asking *questions*.
- They facilitate constant and meaningful *connection*.
- They move us toward greater *collaboration*.
- And they ignite our *creativity*.

As a force shaping everything within digital culture, digital technology subsequently disrupts faith and spiritual practice, demanding change from religious leaders.

It's no secret that the Christian tradition is struggling to find new ways of being the church in a tech-shaped culture. Perhaps you are a leader of a Christian community, trying to make sense of what it means to search for God in a digital age. Perhaps you picked up this book out of a sense of frustration. Maybe the pews are emptier with each passing week, the membership rolls declining, the budgets dwindling. You've done everything in your power to reverse these unsettling trends. You've attended conferences, read books, hired consultants, but the declines continue, nonetheless. You have a story that the world so desperately needs to hear—a message of hope for an age of cynicism, a word of unity for a time of political and social division, a story of healing for a time of pandemic illness. But that story is going unheard, and it's one that is often misunderstood.

This book is about providing you with the clarity and vision to understand what it means to tell God's story in a culture shaped by digital tech—to tell the story in a way that will be heard. This book is also about asking for your help. The church needs people like you to step up and make space for questions. It needs leaders who can form connections in both physical space and cyberspace, and foster creativity and collaboration throughout the community.

Achieving clarity and vision for the church within our tech-shaped culture is not about launching a polished website, starting a hip new social media strategy, or building a trendy mobile app. While this book talks about specific platforms and tools, this is not a book about technological tactics for growing Christian communities. Many such books already exist—some more relevant and prescient than others. Among the best of them is Keith Anderson and Elizabeth Drescher's *Click-2Save Reboot: The Digital Ministry Reboot*. That is the resource you need if you are searching for a reference on starting a church blog, launching a church podcast, or curating a spiritually driven Instagram feed. It's the playbook that every pastor and church leader should have on their shelf. The tactics of digital age engagement are important—and those called to leadership in the church would do well to stay current on the latest tools for digital engagement. Yet fluency in current technology is an ever-changing standard. With the rapid pace of innovation in collaborative and connective technology, it's likely that what was current as I began to write this book will no longer be relevant by its publication.

While fluency in current technology will benefit a church leader for a fleeting moment, deep engagement with the shared values of digital culture will strengthen Christian communities in both the near and distant future. This is a book about the intentional work of cultural transformation to which God is calling the church. Churches can fulfill their mission in a digital age with means that are high-tech, low-tech, and no-tech. Churches can serve God and neighbor with a polished technological presence—or with very little engagement with technology. It doesn't matter what apps congregants use, whether a pastor maintains an updated social feed, if the preacher has a podcast, or if the community gathers in virtual reality. Digital tactics will come and go. The digital tools of today will be the archaic relics of tomorrow. But the cultural values of the digital age will be the values of generations to come.

Culture ought to matter to church leaders because it shapes and reflects the ways we make meaning. Still, as churches have committed to becoming more culturally engaged for the purpose of proclaiming the Gospel to a world of many cultures, leaders tend to misunderstand culture as something of a fixed attribute. Their assumption is that "culture" is something individuals and communities "possess," a list of qualitative communal characteristics that must be considered and accommodated for church to be effective. But culture is not about attributes. Culture is a process of meaning-making by which we come to learn, know, and believe.

Digital culture has a process of meaning-making that differs from cultures that preceded it. Mary Hess, professor of educational leadership at Luther Seminary, teaches several courses on ministry in digital culture for emerging church leaders. According to Hess:

> Within digital culture, the way we come to know something has changed. How we come to understand ourselves and how we come to be in relationship has changed. Since God is known through relationships, the way we come to understand God has changed as well. To do ministry in digital culture, we need a better understanding of these changes.[3]

Being the church in digital culture is not about better technology use. It's about engaging with culture. It is critical for church leaders to study the way that the digital age continues to change meaning-making. What matters now, and what will long continue to matter, is whether those concerned with the future of the Christian tradition think deeply and respond intentionally to these changing ways of knowing. Leaders, lay and ordained, must engage this new set of cultural values if Christian practices and proclamations are ever to resonate with those living in networked communities. Ultimately, if we who care about the sustainability of the Jesus movement fail to adapt to this dynamic process of meaning-making, our ministries are headed for an early ending. Our churches will meet the same fate as PalmPilots, MySpace, and AOL.

From knowing toward searching

The misalignment between the values of digital culture and the experience of church is well-documented in generational cohort data. The more immersed the generation is in digital technology, the less engaged that generation is with church. There is, in fact, a noticeable lack of institutional religiosity in the millennial generation, a cohort of "digital natives" accustomed to constant internet access. Approximately one-third of American millennials consider themselves to be religious "Nones,"[4] a name that refers to their lack of affiliation with organized religion. As these generations began to reach adulthood, between 2007 and 2014, many Christian denominations lost thirty-three to thirty-four percent of their membership.[5] Some have forecast that as these trends accelerate, entire mainline denominations may fold by 2041.[6] Given these data, it would be easy to assume that millennials and subsequent digitally-immersed generations are dismissive of Christian practice. At times, I have joined in this assumption. On many Sunday mornings when I was in my twenties, I worshiped at churches where I was the only twenty-something in attendance. However, this widely shared assumption conflicts with the data about the depth of spirituality in a tech-shaped culture. In the digital age, faith has changed, but it has not declined.

According to The Pew Research Center's 2010 study "Religion Among the Millennials," this younger generation believes in God at a rate that is nearly identical to that of Generation X (those born between 1965 and 1980), the Baby Boomers (those born between 1946 and 1964), and both the Silent and Greatest generations (born between 1928 and 1945, and before 1928, respectively). Millennials' willingness to believe in God carries over to a commitment to individual spiritual practices that take place outside the walls of the institutional church. Millennial Nones and affiliated Christians alike exhibit similar rates of engagement with daily prayer as preceding generations. In 2010, forty-five percent of millennial adults, then ages 18–29, prayed daily. Twenty-seven percent read scripture weekly, and twenty-six percent meditated weekly[7]—all rates of participation equal to or only slightly less than rates of other generations. I am reminded of my generation's spiritual inclinations each time I walk past office meditation rooms, a fixture at tech companies across the country. The Pew Research data suggest that the chief difference between those who came of age in the digital era and those who came of age before lies in institutional affiliation—not in spiritual practices or religious beliefs. Our tech-shaped culture is not turning its back on faith in God so much as it is turning its back on an institution that has been reluctant to to innovate.

From a tech-using to a tech-shaped culture

In writing this book, I set out to simplify the seemingly complex intersection of tech, culture, and religion. Part memoir, part field guide, this book intends to raise up a dialogue and to ignite a conversation about the transformations needed in the ministries of a tech-shaped culture. I wrote this book to help you think about what church leadership and spiritual practice might look like in our hyper-connected landscape. This book invites those connected with a church—whether they be pastors or staff, members or visitors, active or passive participants— to ask questions about what it means to carry on the 2,000-year-old Christian witness into this era of rapid change.

Each of the four sections in this book details one of the values of a tech-shaped culture: questions, connection, collaboration, and creativity. Each section defines the specific value in detail, traces its technological origins, and tells the stories of dynamic ministries and ministry leaders that have adopted these values. Each section includes high-tech, low-tech, and no-tech practices for engaging these cultural values.

Section One: Questions. Digital technologies, particularly search engines, establish a cultural value of learning through questions, conversations, and inquiries. This section explores the incongruence between this cultural value and current ways of being the church. In particular, Christian education remains a process of communicating answers to questions that communities are not asking, while minimizing dialogue and implicitly suppressing questions. I explore how church leaders can facilitate the asking of questions, and in doing so, help their communities to encounter Christ.

Section Two: Connection. Messaging applications like Gmail, WhatsApp, and Snapchat push us toward a cultural norm of "hybrid" connections that seamlessly integrate offline and online experiences. In a tech-shaped culture, connection is about forming new ties, integrating virtual and in-person experiences, and seeing the whole person. I explore how ministries are leaning into hybrid connection, and I tell stories of new forms of high- and low-tech connection in the world of church.

Section Three: Collaboration. This section explores how platforms for digital content creation, including Google Docs, have elevated the importance of shared experiences. Drawing on my career in instructional design, I write about learning as a collaborative exercise and what it would mean for churches to prioritize collaboration in faith formation and in church leadership. At the root of this transformation is a strategic blurring of the lines between teacher and student, lay leadership and clergy, parishioners and visitors—and a commitment to seeing all involved in a ministry as co-collaborators.

Section Four: Creativity. Visually immersive technologies like Instagram, Blogger, and YouTube have given us all the tools to be artists and creators. In the digital age, everyone is the writer, cinematographer, and director of their own life stories—especially their stories of faith. All learning, including faith formation, includes an expectation that we have the role of co-creator. The section looks at how ministries can engage their communities not as content consumers, but as collaborators in telling God's story. Creativity is a messy and unpredictable process. I tell stories of creative successes and creative flops in both the world of technology and the world of church, and I describe what Christian communities would look like if they functioned as workshops for the spiritual practice of creativity.

Throughout each section, I'll draw on personal stories from my career in the technology industry, my years as a seminarian, and my own upbringing in the Christian tradition. I'll also draw on the stories of ministry innovators who have integrated the values of questions, connections, collaborations, and creativity with the proclamation of the Gospel. I know my stories and experiences are similar to many of those who have stood at the imaginary corner of faith and Facebook. It is my hope that you can see yourself in these stories—not as a passive participant, but as a collaborator and co-creator of a story just beginning to unfold.

In the digital age, there are plenty of apps, podcasts, and blogs—though we could always use another. What the church needs is the capacity and will to transform our ministries to engage a culture whose ways of thinking, decision-making, and relating to one another have most certainly changed. As a church insider, I have long observed how church leaders view digital technology as a tactic. It's past time to recognize this new wave of technology for what it is: a revolution that is transforming culture—calling the church to new ways of being.

SECTION 1
QUESTIONS

· ·

As a millennial and a lifelong Lutheran, I have seen how minis-try leaders have struggled with the transition to a tech-shaped culture. Subsequently, I have seen how a lack of innovation by those same leaders has alienated generations of digital natives. I went through confirmation instruction in Appleton, Wisconsin, while in seventh through ninth grades. The year I was confirmed, 2004, was perhaps the highpoint in that congregation's recent history. Mem-bership was the highest it had ever been. The sanctuary had just been remodeled, and well over one hundred youth were going through the confirmation program. The church was putting on musical produc-tions, variety shows, and gourmet dinners, all the while hosting one of the largest and most engaged youth groups in the city.

By my standard, the congregation was booming. While it had recently extended a job offer to a second pastor, everyone knew that the long-tenured senior pastor was the church's true authority. The senior pastor was beginning his fourth decade of ministry at that church. With a loud, booming voice that as a preschooler I would equate with the voice of God itself, this pastor was the leader, the decider, the spiritual guide of the congregation—a twentieth-century model of strong and effective pastoral leadership. He was the communicator of religious truths, the broadcaster of facts, the polished presenter of information about what God was up to in our community. True to the cultural values that preceded the digital age, he was the trained and highly skilled voice who preached a decisive word while the community sat in rapt attention.

A few years after I graduated from high school and moved away from this church, his retirement led to a period of prolonged congregational uncertainty and ambiguity—a sure testament to the breadth and depth of his profound influence over this northeast Wisconsin church. He was an impressive leader of a different era, when pastors acted more as chief executives than as one leader among many sharing ministry responsibilities. His success came from a time when pastors and parishioners alike believed expected information to flow in a straight, hierarchical line from the pulpit to the parish, from expert to audience, from preacher to congregant. The leadership model from which he operated, for its own time, was highly effective in growing and sustaining this church. So why exactly would the youth who grew up in this successful, vibrant setting leave for college and never return? Why would the classrooms of this visibly engaging confirmation program eventually turn out, among those with whom I have kept in touch, more self-identified atheists than church-affiliated Christians?

To find the answers to these questions, it's helpful to step into the Christian education classroom of my youth. Crammed into the fellowship hall, a multipurpose room with ample tables, chairs, and space for potlucks, I remember sitting beside my fellow middle-schoolers for weekly lessons with this senior pastor. The dozens of us who sat in that fellowship hall with our pastor-in-chief were awed by his presence, impressed by his credentials, and slightly afraid of looking naïve or uninformed. This was a man who inspired a sense of reverence and whose leadership style commanded respect. Each Wednesday night, he led us through some central teaching of the Lutheran tradition—the scriptures, the sacraments, the catechism. "What is baptism?" his voice boomed. One of us raised our hand, trying to answer the question through the crackling, squeaky voice of an awkward twelve-year-old. We offered some attempt at an answer, though not being an expert in the creeds and confessions of the church, the class seldom knew the "right" answer. "Baptism!" his voice thundered. "Is being joined to Christ's death and resurrection. It means your sins are forgiven!"

Those in that classroom took the pastor's answers at his word. Nobody in the class was so bold as to challenge the pastor's definition, and few were willing to ask questions other than the ones he provided for us. Out of great respect and reverence, we scribbled his answers in the margins of our Bibles, furiously taking notes on almost everything he told us. None in the class were brave enough to question why an adolescent would care about death and resurrection, or why our sins needed to be forgiven.

But sharing in our desire to be rewarded with cash-filled cards on Confirmation Day, we kept these questions to ourselves. There was one answer that we needed to learn in this church classroom—the answer coming from the sonorous voice in the pulpit, the closest approximation we all had to the voice of the divine. The pastor's pedagogical approach kept our middle-school selves glued to our seats, attentive, engaged, and clinging to every word. But as we all grew up and grew apart from the church of our youth, something about the Christian messages from our upbringing clashed with our experience as adults. Even though my confirmation cohort undoubtedly experienced the church of the 1990s at its best, something about our faith failed to stick. We learned the facts, but we didn't learn how to think theologically in a way that would resonate in the digital age. We learned the creeds, but we didn't develop the capacity for reimaging what church could be in a tech-shaped culture. When I think about the close friends who sat next to me on those Wednesday nights, it alarms me to realize that I may be the only one still sitting in a pew on Sunday mornings.

So, what happened?

1

Asking Our Own Questions

My confirmation class had deep roots in that northeast Wisconsin congregation. Most in my confirmation class were also my classmates in the church's Sunday school and preschool programs. So why do so many of the most deeply rooted students now feel so removed from the Christian faith?

Perhaps I'm still around the church because I was such a difficult Sunday school student. I rather disliked going to Sunday school. Actually, "disliked" is too passive a word. I loathed going to Sunday school, which is surprising given that I enjoyed the mandated, secular schooling that took place Monday through Friday. I loved my elementary school, where there was recess and pizza lunch and plenty of talk about Brett Favre and the Green Bay Packers. But to be dragged from the comfort of my home and the electronic allure of NFL pregame coverage for what seemed like optional learning about Jesus was too much for my young mind to tolerate. There I would sit, in a full classroom of other kids in their Sunday best (often khakis and Packer jerseys), for the longest hour of my week. I wasn't especially well-behaved. I wasn't particularly engaged. I certainly wasn't happy. Today, I frequently get a good laugh from the irony that someone who despised Sunday school as much as I did would go on to

17

four years of seminary. Seminary, of course, is a longer, more intense version of Sunday school, much of it taught in Greek and Hebrew.

Why did I have such disdain for Sunday school? Why did I—a kid who loved learning with the colorful books, the fizzy experiments, the intricate puzzles on weekdays—shut myself off to learning at 9:30 a.m. on Sunday? When I look back on my experience, my dislike of Sunday school may have been the result of the required "memory work." The church expected students in each grade to memorize certain scriptures, creeds, or commandments. If you completed your "memory work," the teacher would give you a prize—a small toy, some candy, or even a doughnut. If you failed to complete it, you got nothing. I had to memorize John 3:16 and the Apostle's Creed, Luther's explanation of the Ten Commandments, and the names of the books of the Bible. The teachers tasked the class with memorizing the names of the prophets and rattling off the twelve disciples. I apparently had a much easier experience than other Sunday school students of the mid-1990s. My wife recalls memorizing all of Luther's *Small Catechism*. Even though she hasn't been to seminary, she can still recite the Apostles' Creed from memory. I still cannot—even with a seminary degree.

Already resistant to the very idea of Sunday school, I did my best not to memorize anything. I wanted to ask questions and learn by doing. I wanted to talk—too much, apparently—and maybe do some running around in the process. I didn't want to learn by memorizing someone else's answers. I wanted to learn by pestering the teachers and pastors with questions. My idea of learning about God didn't quite fit with the ideas of those who built our Sunday school curriculum.

Jesus Christ, who are you?

Somehow, despite my objections to Sunday school, I remained involved in that church—attending youth group, traveling on mission trips, and even volunteering with vacation Bible school. When I was in high school, the church put on a production of Andrew Lloyd Webber's rock opera, *Jesus Christ Superstar*. I was not much for singing or dancing or acting. But I knew that the production needed all the cast members they could recruit from our congregation. When I heard the directors were seeking someone to play the part of "Roman Guard Number Two," I decided it was time to make my off-off-Broadway debut. With my offensive lineman frame, I figured I was a perfect fit for the role. Plus, I was going to get the chance to carry a spear and eat free pizza at the rehearsals—not a bad deal for a growing high schooler. As a cast member, my main role was to look angry and intimidating, while managing not to scare the small children in attendance. It was also my job to join the cast backstage as a member of the chorus during the show-stopping finale from which the musical gets its name. When the vocals of the actor playing the role of Judas cut out, those of us in the chorus would sing into a microphone: "Jesus Christ, Jesus Christ, who are you? What have you sacrificed?" That production represented the first time I recognized the centrality of questions to the life of faith, even questions sung in a Broadway-style refrain. I would later realize that those in our tech-shaped culture were asking these types of questions with ever-growing frequency. Americans, in particular, increasingly find themselves asking Andrew Lloyd Weber's and Pontius Pilate's (played in my church's production by my very own father) evergreen question: just who, exactly, is Jesus?

And they're doing it on search engines more often with each passing year, especially around Christmas and Easter.[1] According to its own trends data, Google saw three times as many searches for the query "who is Jesus?" in Christmas 2017 than in Christmas 2007. It's a question that grows in volume every year in every state. It is a question that is among the most frequently "Googled" religious queries, second only to "what is the Bible?"[2] The "Googling" of Christ's identity and the significance of the Bible points to an accelerating trend: people are developing their faith through questions. They are developing their spiritual selves not through passive consumption of facts, but through active inquiry. They are, in every sense, searching for God with Google.

The importance of asking

A few years after appearing in *Jesus Christ Superstar*, I would again realize the connection between questions and digital-age faith, this time while in the deep woods of Waupaca, Wisconsin—miles from screens and cell coverage. In these woods, I spent the summers of my college years working as a counselor at Pine Lake Camp. The camp is a Lutheran outdoor ministry situated on over one hundred pristine acres, with a sparkling lake, a dense pine forest, and over a dozen cabins where hundreds of kids spend part of their summer.

Each day at camp includes three shared meals, plenty of time for play and recreation, some Bible study, and a bit of worship. At the end of the day, I would lead my cabin group in a brief devotional reflection—usually something having to do with God's presence in the silence of nature. After I read the reflection, I would do my best to facilitate a conversation based on slips of paper campers had dropped in the cabin's "question box." The question box was a shoebox covered with colorful paper, and it had a narrow slit for anonymous, written questions. The questions could be about anything, but because we were at a Christian camp, most of the questions were related to faith and spirituality. Some questions were theologically complex, yet somewhat comical. "If there is a God, how come there are poisonous berries that grow in these woods?" asked one fifth-grade camper. "Why did Satan invent mosquitoes?" asked a middle schooler who had forgotten to put on bug spray prior to the day's nature hike. "My aunt died of cancer. Did Jesus love her?" asked a high school student grieving over the loss of a close relative.

As camp counselors, we likely had more training in first aid and fire building than theology, but we did our best to humbly respond to the questions. We attempted to reflect the question back to the campers, asking them to articulate their ideas, affirming their thoughts, and encouraging them to keep asking. I don't know where these campers are nearly one decade later. I pray they're well. I hope they love the outdoors. I imagine that they don't remember what I taught them about stewardship or redemption in Bible study. But I am sure they remember those evening question-box sessions. I am nearly certain that they can still recall those solemn and sacred moments—the dimmed lights, the bunks illuminated only by flashlight—those moments when their questions flowed as freely as the Spirit.

Removed from the digital distractions of phones and computers for a week, the campers at Pine Lake taught me that in a tech-shaped culture, questions are an indicator that somebody is learning. Learning in the digital age is about asking authentic, timely, and candid questions. We learn best when the information we receive addresses the questions we are truly asking. We learn rather poorly when the information we receive addresses questions of indifference. Questions about God resonated with those young minds. Camp provided a setting that affirmed their questions, showing them that if we want to know who Jesus is, we first have to ask. There is a time and a place for the questions and answers of catechism class. But in a digital age, that time must be brief, and that place must be set among opportunities to ask the questions of one's search for God.

For reflection and discussion

- What specific questions have you asked in your personal faith journey?

- To what extent would you feel comfortable asking those questions in a church?
- Why do you think churches have be perceived as closed off to questions and curiosity?

Making space for questions: ideas for youth ministry	
High-tech	Using video conferencing software, connect with a youth ministry in a different city, state, or country. Meet regularly to ask questions of one another to explore the diverse expressions of the life of faith.
Low-tech	Create a "virtual questions box" using an app like Google Forms. Encourage youth to submit anonymous questions about faith and life at any time.
No-tech	Demonstrate the importance of questions to the life of faith. On a semi-recurring class, such as in a confirmation class or youth group gathering, invite an adult member of the congregation to share a few thoughts about the questions, concerns, or doubts that they have encountered along their faith journey.

2

The Past:
A Church that
Silences Questions

The rise of the importance of questions in our culture parallels the rise of the search engine. In today's search engine-driven world, it is seldom necessary to memorize facts. We assume asking questions is our prerogative and that answers are available. To learn something is to understand how to ask the relevant questions in the right context. We no longer look to accept answers from only one source or authority. We instead expect to evaluate the many possible choices that align to our questions.

When a user asks a question on Google, seldom are they given a tidy single answer. Rather, Google gives them a litany of possible answers to their question. Most questions are met with millions of potential answers, spread across seemingly endless results pages. Search engines, both standalone versions like Google and the engines embedded into most apps and websites, make life easy by applying an apparently objective algorithm to the search results page, stack ranking the answers in terms of relevance, originality, quality, and frequency of use. This is the reason my queries about the first moon landing were met with links to

NASA, the History Channel, and the Air and Space Museum. I assume the fringe conspiracy theories about falsified lunar landings were buried deep among the seventy-five million available results.

Few searches can in fact be addressed with a single answer. If I ask for the temperature right now in Madison, Wisconsin, Google tells me it is precisely forty-two degrees Fahrenheit—an empirical measurement sent to the search engine by digitally integrated technology at the Dane County Airport. If I ask for movie showtimes tonight, Google tells me that I can see *Avengers Endgame* this evening at 7:05 p.m.—an objective and inscrutable fact that is validated by dozens of movie-listing websites, including Fandango, Atom Tickets, and New Vision Theatres. Yet through all its search listings, the overarching paradigm is a user's ability to select from multiple answers to questions they have asked.

Not all of Google's suggested outcomes are equal; many are far more authoritative than others. But when a search engine responds to my questions about the first moon landing with seventy-five million possible answers, it conditions me to think about the pursuit of knowledge not as something with a fixed and definitive endpoint but as a process of questioning with a vast array of paths, choices, and endpoints. Subtly, search technology is tempering the expectation that questions have a single answer, chipping away at the notion that one should rely exclusively on a single authority.

If we want to observe how search engines influence our thoughts, we should observe the companies that create these technologies. As a firm, Google goes to great lengths to convince new employees to buy-in to their mission to "organize the world's information and make it universally accessible and useful." Implicit in the ambitious statement is a quality of unfinishedness. It describes the company's unending quest to gather information and assemble it into a format that is coherent yet malleable, accurate yet respective of context, authoritative yet amenable to possibility. Universal accessibility and usability are unreachable and ever-evolving standards that demand constant calibration, reflection, and frankly, a considerable amount of questioning. To achieve that standard is to constantly sift through and experiment with many questions and countless answers in an unceasing journey of improvement. To thrive at a company like Google is to understand that your perspective is a necessary yet fragmentary part of a dynamic whole, a unique node in a vast network of knowledge.

Former Google chairman Eric Schmidt describes in his bestseller, *How Google Works,* why "a multiplicity of viewpoints—aka diversity— is your best defense against myopia."[1] According to this perspective, we develop a more complete comprehension by including questions and divergent perspectives into a rich mosaic of awareness and knowing. Part of building this mosaic of knowledge involves expanding the number of voices and perspectives in the conversation, ensuring more questions are asked and more answers are offered. Organizations that are committed to this type of knowing develop open systems of knowing that facilitate social and organizational good. Decisions in these systems, made with respect to more opinions and experiences, are less susceptible to individual bias. These systems are less beholden to charismatic and persuasive individuals, as they include more qualitative and quantitative data with which to draw conclusions.

To thrive in the organizational world of the digital age is to understand that knowledge has a rather unpredictable flow in which all interested parties are entitled to question, to answer, and to seek understanding together. Organizations like Google succeed in tech-shaped culture because they democratize information access and usage. These companies provide their teams transparent access to information so it can be quickly acted upon to solve business challenges. By embracing the free flow of questions and answers, these companies can convert many questions into attunement and awareness, and many perspectives into intelligence and innovation.

Perspectives are never expanded out of some need for political correctness, as some cynics might suggest, but out of the realization that expansive perspectives are required for the digital age organization to fulfill its mission. In my career, I've seen the careers of colleagues without great technical aptitude soar when they consciously prioritize collaboration and multiple perspectives. I've also seen highly talented colleagues stumble when they've taken too aggressive a stand and dismissed their colleagues' questions as unimportant, as if their own point of view represented an exclusive source of truth.

Google's commitment to asking questions and expanding perspectives is visible each week at its employee all-hands event. The meeting, known as "TGIF," even though the meeting itself is now held on Thursdays, is a low-tech yet candid question-and-answer session. Google's senior leaders take the stage in a cafeteria at company headquarters to provide updates on the latest company news—and to take unfiltered, unmoderated questions from the audience. Whether you are sitting in the crowd in California or dialed into the meeting from Google's offices around the globe, you can ask anything of the company's top executives, including co-founders Larry Page and Sergey Brin and current CEO Sundar Pichai. Employees often ask rather critical questions; it's a meeting, after all, not a fan club gathering. Some of the questions can trigger intense debates, especially during controversial news cycles. I sat in the audience at TGIF for particularly heated conversations over controversial new policies for platforms like YouTube and Blogger, and controversial decisions to remove popular products. But even the most heated question-and-answer sessions affirmed that successful organizations value asking questions and engaging multiple perspectives.

The tech industry is a microcosm of digital culture's preference for learning through questions. Our ability to thrive, as individuals and as organizations, is predicated on our willingness to connect our perspectives with other experiences to build a more complete understanding.

Intelligence is not measured by the volume of our knowledge, but by the fluency with which one can ask, answer, and reflect as part of a greater network.

A church with too few answers

As search engine technology has presented people with opportunities to ask countless questions and evaluate many possible answers, leadership and learning have become increasingly participatory. Teaching has transitioned from a hierarchical model centered on a single authority to a networked model predicated on the shared knowledge and inquisitiveness of community.[2]

Organizations that have achieved their goals in a tech-shaped culture don't experience their success because they unite their teams behind a single point of view. They are the organizations that unify their teams behind a common mission while empowering individuals to ask questions, generate alternative ideas, and push back on tenuous answers.

Contrast that process to the world of religion. Among the unchurched, the perception of Christianity is that of a group that claims to have a monopoly on inscrutable spiritual truth. Accurate or not, the perception exists that pastors and other religious leaders answer questions with a single option, take it or leave it. In too many situations, if you choose the leave-it option, your only recourse is to find a different church or, as I have seen in my friends' experiences, to stop showing up all together. Church leaders present religious information in ways that are seldom varied or diverse, ways that implicitly stifle or leave little room for the questions in the community.

The most revered form of communication, especially in the Protestant tradition, is that of a sermon preached by an ordained minister. In this environment, questions are met with one answer, that of the preacher. Answers are presented in one format, that of the didactic word. And the perspective presented is often limited to that of the pastor. If Christian leadership is to reverse the narrative of decline amidst digital culture, it must embrace the value of the question—while loosening the grip on the answers. Leaders must expand the perspectives that are proclaimed and increase the number of voices who can proclaim them.

I have long observed, both as an inquisitive youth and now as an adult, that church leaders are often uneasy around questions and ambiguity—around not having the right answer. While I hope questions are more welcomed than when I first joined a youth group, I have seen youthful curiosity met with the theological thunderbolts of well-meaning yet intellectually aggressive adults. I have too often seen church leaders play the religious education trump card with questioners of all ages. Too often, I have seen leaders apply their master's degrees to pull rank over the heartfelt, well-intentioned questions and musings of Christians, much to the spiritual detriment of those searching for God in a digital age.

Having volunteered to teach and assist with confirmation programs since high school, I know how impossibly frantic the lives of these students have become. It is not unusual for my students to show up to class while scarfing down a burrito, having gone to school, practiced baseball, picked up dinner, and showed up at church—just for a couple of hours before they are whisked off to basketball practice! Those of us in the church should never stop celebrating that these students show up in the first place. Leaders owe it to them, and to everyone who shows up, regardless of age or background or experience, to provide a space where their many questions are celebrated—and taken seriously. Ample space for questions is a prerequisite to faith formation for people of all ages in our tech-shaped culture.

I'm not suggesting that Christian leadership is never about providing answers or input. The challenge confronting the church does not come from providing answers but from the tone in which these answers are provided. As digital culture becomes more accustomed to learning through questions, people will increasingly resist encumberment. Those living in a tech-shaped culture value that which expands the conversation and oppose that which seeks to end the conversation altogether. Too many priests and pastors address spiritual questions in a form that resembles a theological jab, as if they are trying to knock the question out with a well-landed intellectual punch. The leaders of the digital age church leader must soften their approach. They can still communicate answers, they can still proclaim their interpretation of the Gospel, they can still hold on to their doctrine or brochure-length belief statements. Making space for questions is first and foremost about providing answers in a tone that continues, rather than concludes, the dialogue.

In many church circles, even the suggestion that more than one explanation for a spiritual question might exist can trigger the animosity of the community. Christian leaders become defensive if you imply that their understanding of the mystery that is God is incomplete. In some of the Christian circles that I have been part of, a simple question about the meaning of the cross, the reality of the bodily resurrection, or even the need for God's forgiveness can set off a cascade of accusations about the sincerity and validity of one's beliefs. Religion is markedly efficient at producing doctrinal statements on metaphysics. If only church leaders, who seem to insist more on compliance than on conversation, were more efficient at making space for questions.

Frequently one to call into question others' assumptions revealed on social media, I've often been reminded that I am out of compliance with the powerful voices of broadcast Christianity. In my adult years, I have been called a relativist on Facebook, I have been called subjective on Twitter, and I have been accused of not taking scripture "seriously" by pastors right in my hometown. A questions-based process for learning is evidently difficult to achieve in the world of church.

While I was studying at the University of Wisconsin–Madison, the Department of Religious Studies invited theologian Jim Wallis to campus for a forum on interfaith dialogue. As a church nerd, I was thrilled to attend his events. I was intrigued by his reputation as a progressive theologian, a widely known Christian leader who cares about immigrants, refugees, and those with experiences different from his. I had long been a follower of his *Sojourners* platform, a prolific magazine and online publication that engages faith, culture, and politics. I was also interested in having the chance to discuss the varied campus experience of Christian, Muslim, and Jewish students.

At one of his events, a question came from a student I had met at other gatherings of the campus faith community, a student who distributes brochures on attaining eternal salvation in just four steps—the kind of student who would zealously invite you to a Saturday night Bible study, attempting to dissuade you from an evening of debauchery and red Solo cups. In college, I was all about the Bible—as long as it didn't come between me, an ice-cold beer, and a slice of late-night pizza. This student opened the conversation by politely asking how Wallis could sincerely engage interfaith work without "compromising his truth claims."

Implicitly, I knew what he was asking. Would sitting down for a conversation with a Muslim student somehow affirm the possibility of speaking of God in more than one way? Could a dialogue with a Jewish student somehow open the door to the heretical idea that one could discern God's action in the world apart from the mediation of Jesus Christ? Wouldn't interfaith dialogue imply that each of our perspectives on God is limited by our social location? I do not remember how Wallis answered the question, though I suspect Wallis' interfaith work continues, while the interfaith work of the questioner never began. When Christians turn their backs on questions, they don't just fail to adapt to the shape of the digital age, they fail to empathize with the experience of their neighbor. In failing to empathize, Christians lose the opportunity to engage the neighbor's questions in a broader conversation on life's biggest questions.

It's clearly not easy for Christians, American Christians in particular, to balance the diversity of meaning inherent in a tech-shaped culture with the tradition's deeply rooted fears of inaccuracy. I am not suggesting a need to welcome every conceivable opinion with arms wide open; the church is entitled to its doctrines. But if Christians are to avoid sliding into cultural irrelevance, it's imperative for leaders to find a way to give people the necessary space to sit with and express their raw, open, and fragmentary ideas—and questions.

For reflection and discussion

- When and where have you encountered a church leader who appeared closed-off or even hostile towards questions?
- What do you think made them uncomfortable with questions?
- When and where have you encountered a church leader who affirmed the importance of questions?
- How did it feel to encounter a church leader who welcomed and affirmed your questions?

Making space for questions: ideas for faith formation	
High-tech	Create a class podcast. A host invites community members to record a 15-minute audio interview in which they describe why faith is important in their life. The host asks plenty of questions and invites participants to share questions they have about God, the community's life together, or our callings in the world.
Low-tech	"Flip the classroom." Distribute a short video or podcast prior to a faith formation event. When gathered together, use the time not to present but to discuss.
No-tech	Instead of focusing classes on a subject, gather a group to discuss a specific question, like "Why take time for Advent in a culture that skips ahead to Christmas?"

The Future:
A Church that
Celebrates Questions

Christian leaders have the means of making space for questions in their faith communities. For starters, Christian communities need to embrace the idea that digital age learning is about searching, and searching begins with our questions. Sermons by ordained ministers or one-way communication on the radio or television waves expanded the influence of American Christianity when the culture was conditioned to view and accept the teachings of an authority figure. Being granted access to the pulpit or to a television station signified that a voice was credible. Christians were expected not to question the voices of the mighty and the well-connected, but to take their words as, well, gospel. In the previous technological era, faith was formed not by pursuing one's curiosity or questions but by hearing and accepting another's word.

Today, countless learning pursuits begin not with the directive of an expert, but with a question from a seeker. Want to learn to be an active listener? Search for active listening tips, or request guidance from a mentor. Want to learn to write JavaScript? Search for a free Java-Script course, or seek out tips from a friend or colleague. Interested in learning how to play the guitar? Ask any online search engine for a good guitar tabs resource, or connect with the guitarists at your local music store. Learning in both online and offline settings is now about two-way communication, mutual questions, and shared contributions to the answer. What edifies us now is not our act of listening, but our act of questioning.

It's unsurprising that those in digital culture are fluent in questioning. Outside of church, our culture encourages questions. In my experience, though, people both inside and outside the institutional church are deeply uncomfortable articulating questions about faith and spirituality. Explicitly or implicitly, church leaders have discouraged the act of questioning. As those in our tech-shaped culture have come to view churches as places where questions are not welcome, people are asking their questions outside of the church, often taking their inquiries about faith and spirituality to search engines.

What would it look like for a church community to be the facilitators of sacred questions and not keepers of inscrutable truths? For the Jesus movement to thrive in this cultural moment, it is first necessary to sacralize the question, not just the sermon. Religious leaders have an obligation to make space for the question mark—even if it means dealing with questions that might seem a bit unusual.

Church begins with the Spirit gathering individuals together. As a body of individuals, the pivot towards a church that asks more questions begins at the individual level. Individuals, church leaders in particular, need to find a way to verbalize the questions they have long been expected to suppress. Spiritual seekers inside and outside the church will find value in articulating spiritual questions as they come up. I encourage church leaders to carry a notebook, or download a note-taking app like Google Keep or Evernote, for the purposes of recording questions about God, religion, and spirituality. In this busy life, we can never quite predict when and where the big questions of being will emerge.

I find myself contemplating such questions when I'm bored during a meeting—usually a church committee meeting that could just as easily have been an email exchange. I also seem drawn to these questions while I'm camping, miles away from the distractions of social media and email. I tend to note these questions on my phone as they arise, not so much to remind myself to search for a specific answer, but train myself in the spiritual discipline of the question. In the digital age, spiritual practice involves raising awareness around those questions and bringing those questions into a broader conversation. We who care about ministry in a digital age need to train ourselves to participate in the new networks of learning.

Increasing our awareness of such questions helps us to recognize the importance of curiosity to the life of faith. By simply writing questions down, you train your mind to exhibit greater curiosity. You condition yourself for the search. As the spiritual discipline of the question becomes habitual, you'll soon recognize that asking questions, as important as it is to our spiritual well-being, functions as a mental muscle. Like any muscle, it needs exercise. Like the strongest weight lifters or the fastest marathoners, the deepest spiritual thinkers of the digital age will be those who train to ask the constant question. In the digital age, churches need to be facilitators of the sacred question, not keepers of the inscrutable truth. So start asking—and may your community hear you with open ears and open minds.

How to cultivate questions

Making space for questions isn't easy. It takes intentionality to cultivate such space. It takes discipline and humility. And it takes considerable planning. To understand what it means for a church to become more affirming of questions, I sat down for a conversation with Pastor Stephanie Williams O'Brien, a pastor, podcaster, and the author of *Stay Curious:*

How Questions and Doubts Can Save Your Faith. O'Brien believes that asking questions and wondering about God is central to a life of faith, and ought to be central to the work of the church. For O'Brien, this work begins with making one's church a "brave space" for asking questions.

"People don't need permission to be curious about God. Still, it's helpful for church leaders to affirm that you can always ask questions," says O'Brien, who encourages pastors and preachers to consistently invite and affirm questions from their community.[1] "Give them permission to disagree," she says. "Remind the community that it's OK not to be on the same page as the preacher. Remind them that we're seeking Jesus, and that seeking is an expression of curiosity."

O'Brien also encourages church leaders to center the community's life together in curiosity through the repeated use of a big question. She regularly invites those who gather at Mill City Church, her congregation in Minneapolis, Minnesota, to ask the question, "What is God doing?" and then, "How can we join in?" By doing so, O'Brien's congregation fuses the asking of questions with the life of discipleship. Such questions are important to Mill City Church's adult education programs, known as "Equipping Hour." Unlike more traditional Sunday school curriculum, "Equipping Hour" is designed as a conversation, not a lesson. "Our teachers are facilitators and wonderers, not lecturers," says O'Brien. "We make plenty of space for learners to ask questions, to interact, and to push back." By emphasizing the question in worship and faith formation, O'Brien's congregation has created a virtuous cycle. Questions about how one can join with what God is doing can lead to a life of faithful action and discipleship. Living out one's faith leads to new questions about what God is doing, which leads to a perpetually active, perpetually curious faith community.

Leaders can create this virtuous cycle of questions and discipleship in any faith community. To start, one might complete a simple communication auditing exercise—what I refer to as a "punctuation analysis"—to determine the extent of change that must take place in order to be facilitators of the sacred question. Such an exercise will determine the degree to which questions are prioritized within the community and will reveal concrete next steps for wondering about God and walking with Christ.

Start by reflecting on the flow of communication in your church. Draw a vertical line in the middle of page. Atop the left side of the page, write "Questions." Atop the right side of the page, write "Answers." Then, think about a recent week in the life of the congregation, or if that's too much, just think about a recent Sunday morning. Note on that left-hand column any time that you have observed a community member—including a pastor or minister—asking a question about God, Jesus, discipleship, or any other faith-related concern. Exclude the practical, logistical questions like "where is the restroom?" or "what time does coffee hour begin?" These questions are important, but they're not the questions that matter to this exercise. List any time someone was given the space to question some teaching, push back against some doctrine, or express concerns about church practice. The number of entries on this side of the ledger reflects the extent to which your ministry exists as a facilitator of questions.

Once you have exhausted these examples, turn to the right-hand side of the page. In that column, note any time you have observed a community member providing an answer about the existence of God, the purpose of suffering, or the reality of evil. They could be answers to explicit questions or questions that have not even been asked. Be diligent because these answers can be hidden. Sermons, newsletters, e-mails, blog posts—these can all be short on questions and long on answers. Document this downward communication, wherever it exists, whether it comes from pastors, deacons, teachers, parishioners, or potluck hosts. Again, exclude the logistical questions. Think only in terms of what is stated as fact, what is expressed as a certitude, what is preached as inscrutable truth.

I would predict that the right-hand side has many more items. I would predict that the group spent more time identifying answers than identifying questions. I would predict that you nearly ran out of space in the right-hand column.

Having completed this brief exercise, this "punctuation audit," you now see the contours of the work in front of you. Start by reflecting on small, incremental change. How could you shift one item on the right-hand column to the left-hand column? What would it take? Supporting this movement could be as simple as changing word usage and phrasing. Be selective in choosing one item, then be deliberate in the change.

What might a Sunday morning at church look like if equal space was provided for the question alongside the answer? Can you select a particular practice that you could use to facilitate dialogue, feedback, and inquiry? Can you add a questions box near the door to the sanctuary? Could you embed a feedback form on your church website or app? Perhaps you could commit to semi-regular breakout conversations as part of the sermon. Or what if, instead of coffee hour conversations on the local sports teams, attendees were invited to share their questions with others who have gathered for worship? Making space for questions on Sunday morning can be a high-tech or low-tech process, involving changes to the liturgy or changes to the physical space of the sanctuary. What matters far more than the method is leaders' and the community's commitment to welcoming questions and their openness to recognizing they are the means by which we in our tech-shaped culture learn about and develop a relationship with God.

For reflection and discussion

- What challenges have you seen with the way churches engage questions? Do you think this presents a problem for being the church in a tech-shaped culture? Why or why not?
- How can a church leader discover the types of questions that matter most to their congregation?
- What pushback might a church leader encounter when attempting to make space for more questions in their community?

Making space for questions: ideas for worship	
High-tech	Use a polling app like Doodle or Poll Everywhere during the sermon. Ask a question, invite worshippers to respond anonymously on their phone, and post the results on a video screen.
Low-tech	Include a discussion question in most social media posts. Encourage the community to react and respond to pictures, videos, and announcements from the community.
No-tech	Integrate questions into the prayers of the people. Invite worshippers to write anonymous questions on slips of paper. The person who crafts the prayers of the people can incorporate such questions into the prayers and offer them up to God. After each question is read, a moment of stillness is observed for contemplation.

SECTION 2
CONNECTION

. . . .

When new employees start a career at tech companies like Google, they might be overwhelmed by the constant-connection cultural norm. It's not that they are expected to be available to coworkers and online at all hours of the day and night—though some overzealous employees might choose this lifestyle. It's more that the world of technology removes much of the buffer between the self and one's peers, and between offline and online experiences. Connecting in a tech-shaped culture is a process of navigating hybrid experiences, where there is little distinction between offline and online.

To visualize what it means to simultaneously connect offline and online, it's helpful to consider the spaces in which many tech companies operate. Their floor plans and furnishings don't include much dedicated space for individuals. For example, my coworkers and I at the Google office in Ann Arbor, Michigan, worked in "pods," a space shared by four coworkers. Each pod had ample room for other coworkers to stop by for a conversation. But with the constant connection to my coworkers and their dogs (always welcome at every Google office), I never felt like I had access to a room of my own. I still work in a completely open office, which lacks any semblance of walls, doors, or other barriers of a bygone era and where desks are strewn throughout the workplace. The arrangement has its advantages. It encourages and

41

facilitates collaboration. It leads to engaging peer-to-peer conversations that may never have happened in a more traditional office setting. Of course, there are disadvantages. Our tech-shaped culture's expectation of hybrid connections have developed not only because tech employees (and increasingly workers in other arenas) are in close physical proximity, however. Apps and tools have made it easy to start a conversation online, to continue face-to-face, and to conclude a conversation with digital technology. Even when I step away from my desk, I'm still connected to my coworkers through communication apps and technologies that make it possible to seamlessly extend conversations.

Messaging tools have made it easy to switch between face-to-face and online connection. These tools—email, chat, Slack, Zoom, and many more with each passing year—are immersive, effective, and perhaps even addicting. Most of us are constantly connected with these tools, frequently if not frenetically. In America, seventy-one percent of us, myself included, sleep within arm's reach of a smartphone.[1] Approximately half of us check our work email in bed—which is only a slightly higher percentage than those of us who check our work email while on vacation. Ten percent of us check our email every single waking hour of a vacation.[2] This constant virtual connection would be tedious and irritating if it didn't allow us to strengthen relationships that often begin in face-to-face encounters. We expect that virtual connections can be just as meaningful as in-person encounters. Connecting meaningfully depends on being available, being authentic, and trusting those on the other side of the screen. It requires a commitment to forming new ties, to integrating the virtual with the physical, and to seeing the whole person across contexts.

As it develops, digital technology increasingly supports more meaningful connection across physical and virtual environments. Messaging tools have evolved from applications for exchanging a few lines of text to platforms for rich interpersonal exchange. Recent innovations in messaging tools, from Gmail to Snapchat to WhatsApp, provide increasingly varied opportunities to build an extensive social network and to bring our full selves into those connections.

Perhaps no single tool has done more to advance the ubiquity of these types of deep hybrid connections than Google's Gmail.[3] As of October 2018, Gmail had over 1.5 billion active users, approximately twenty percent of Earth's human population.[4] Gmail became a platform for constant and meaningful connection because Gmail offered something no other platforms could: nearly unlimited storage. At its onset, Gmail offered over a hundred times the storage space of its competitors—at no cost to the user.[5] In those early days, when email was useful for sporadic, superficial contacts, Google converted email into a platform for developing, maintaining, and extending connections.

Gmail was in many ways the early blueprint for today's messaging tools. Whether reaching out to a colleague on Slack or a friend on WhatsApp, connective technologies are accessible, contextual, and flexible. Through text, visuals, and sound, messaging technologies augment experiences with detail and personality. With technologies like Emoji, which annotates messaging with illustrated reactions, and applications like Bitmoji, which add personalized comics to the messaging thread, connections on such platforms have become increasingly customizable and often more fun.

Digital technology has made it increasingly easy to bring constant and meaningful connections—once the domain of face-to-face encounter—into digital platforms. Today, our deepest connections are a hybrid of online and offline experiences, an amalgamation of the physical and the digital. The question for church leaders in our tech-shaped culture is not just how to connect online, but how to connect in a culture with blurred boundaries between the offline and online experience.

4

Finding New Ways to Connect

I experienced the hybrid pattern of digital age connection not just in the tech industry, but in my theology studies. Theology and software might seem an unlikely pairing, given how many of my seminary class-mates have gone into full-time church employment while few of my "day job" coworkers go to church at all! But I found my studies on mission development, ethics, justice, and servant leadership to comple-ment the technology industry's pace and style of innovation. I have found tech firms to be completely amenable to new ways of thinking, processing, and acting. The tech industry has a strong commitment to justice, diversity, and inclusion—topics covered extensively in semi-nary. It didn't take long for me to discover that good theology, with its insistence on seeing people in their uniqueness and fullness, could offer a great deal to tech. Similarly, it didn't take long for me to realize that hybrid connections could offer a great deal to the Christian witness.

My seminary experience involved four years of consistent study and connection building in a hybrid setting. Those who go through seminary together typically become fast friends on the journey of religious leader-ship. I suspect seminary graduates have always thought of the relation-ships formed through those years as one of the most significant aspects of the experience. Like generations before me, I consider the relationships I formed central to my seminary work. However, my experience differed from earlier seminarians' in one significant way. Aside from a few freezing weeks each year in St. Paul, Minnesota, all of my interaction with classmates was on internet forums, Google Hangouts, and Facebook.

Still, each time we gathered on campus, whether for intensive courses or for commencement ceremonies, I was struck by the depth of our friendships. I've seen online seminary cohorts practically become second families. From regular social media discussions on seminary-specific Facebook pages, to dinner outings during on-campus intensives, to shared celebrations upon graduation and, for some, ordination, my seminary classmates and I built unshakeable connections. And this makes sense—not many people are going through these programs, which are quite academically rigorous and spiritually demanding. We need to lean on one another for support. The strength and vitality of online student networks—in addition to the face-to-face networks enjoyed by earlier generations of seminarians—provides the support one needs to see it through.

Christian seminaries are leading the way in thinking about what it means to be the church in this culture of hybrid connection. "Everything today is a hybrid event," says Sarah Stonesifer Boylan of Virginia Theological Seminary. Stonesifer, Manager of Operations and Digital Missioner, runs trainings, workshops, and meetups for Christian leaders that explore what it means to connect constantly and meaningfully in digital culture. She says:

> The church needs to find a way to live into hybrid space, where relationships are rarely exclusively online or exclusively offline. There are so many people in the church that don't want to engage the electronic format of connections. But the church is called to both. We can't just choose one or the other.[1]

Stonesifer's perspectives on the importance of hybrid connections and digital age religion are shared by scholars of new media and religion. "Faith in the offline world was about relationality and connection," says Heidi Campbell, a Texas A&M professor of communications and a leading scholar of religion and new media.[2] "It's really no different in the digital age. It's still about relationships, it's still about connecting, and it's still about starting conversations."

"Saint Paul used letters to connect people, I use posts on Facebook to do the same," says Campbell. "Creating connections across distances through text across wide geographic distances has always been part of our story. The way the text is created and read has changed. But connection is as important as ever."

Though hybrid connection is an increasingly common cultural experience, many church leaders still assume that Christian communities ought to exist primarily offline. Whether the perception is fair, the church seems to be focused on the connections that form during one hour per week in a face-to-face setting, typically on a Sunday morning. It's unsurprising that church leaders prefer face-to-face encounters, given that such encounters often facilitate meaningful connection. Why venture online, they might ask, when churches are so effective and efficient at creating connections from face-to-face encounters?

Sociological data on churchgoing adults indicate that leaders who prefer to nurture offline connection are at least partially justified in that choice. In *Bowling Alone* (2000), a classic study on American social capital, sociologist Robert Putnam observes that those who regularly attend church services are more likely to donate to charity, volunteer in their community, and engage in other types of activities that build social capital. Spending just an hour or two a week at church has been consistently correlated with engaging in the community and practicing altruism, a finding that has held throughout American religious history.[3]

Walking into the typical American church, it's not difficult to see why. One is likely to see the walls plastered with sign-up sheets and information on upcoming events. One will see bulletin boards adorned with committee reports, framed photos celebrating past in-person events, updates on fundraising drives for clothes closets or food pantries, and signs welcoming church visitors.

At church, strong social capital emerges from a small investment of time. Thirty-six percent of American adults attend church weekly. This means that one-third of Americans invest one hour per week in the church.[4] What's most remarkable about Putnam's data is not that the religiously connected exhibit more consistent prosocial behavior. It's that the prosocial behavior is correlated with so little time spent in a church setting—that one to two hours of connection per week is all that's needed to facilitate altruistic behavior and drive social impact. It seems that what the church lacks in engagement hours it more than makes up for in engagement impact.

Not surprisingly, when speaking with a ministry retiree or a pastor who graduated from seminary decades ago, I often hear skeptical comments regarding the strength of online connection, particularly in the context of the church and theological education. It's not that they don't trust the quality of online theological education. What many pastors from previous generations seem to assume is that the sense of community and connection in a distributed learning cohort must inevitably be superficial and shallow—that the only way to be the church or to study theology is in the face-to-face environment that they are most familiar with.

Given their experience, they think the only way to build connections is to demand seminarians move into a dormitory (or move their families into an apartment) and spend four years conjugating Greek verbs with accomplished academics while enjoying tankards of ale at the local saloon. Some of these skeptics occupy the highest levels of leadership within the Lutheran church, a denomination that still expects seminarians to complete ten academic credits (the equivalent of one academic year) on campus during their seminary studies. Their insistence on giving up one year of one's life for the sake of theological intensive coursework is a decision made from a lack of familiarity with the diversity and strength of connection in a tech-shaped culture and with how connective technologies have erased the distinctions between face-to-face and online connection. Thrust suddenly into the age of messaging technology, some church leaders, especially in the senior ranks of the institution, still don't understand that we can be meaningfully connected without necessarily being in the same space.

Yet as valuable as exclusively face-to-face connections in a church can be, they're happening with decreasing frequency. In 1960, sixty-three percent of us regularly attended a worship service—the highest rate of attendance in American history.[5] In 2019, only thirty-six percent attended regularly, thirty-three percent attended infrequently, and thirty percent did not attend at all.[6] This precipitous drop in attendance will most likely accelerate in the coming years. According to Pew Research, millennials attend service at approximately one-third of the rate of Generation X and baby boomers. As millennials become America's largest generational cohort, they'll have a powerful impact on continued declines in church attendance.

It is irresponsible for church leaders to continue using the same tactics they've used for the past century or more, while hoping that the rapidly growing unchurched and unheard populations will suddenly start showing up on Sundays. Yes, the Christian tradition is deeply rooted in coming together to encounter the grace of God, and Christian communities will likely always value collective, synchronous connection. The digital age does not demand that faith communities deprioritize being together at the same time in the same space. Rather, it calls the stewards of the tradition to find new ways of gathering offline and online.

The cultural reality of the digital age is that meaningful connections are hybrid connections. If the church, an institution dedicated to relationality and accompaniment, is to thrive in a culture without much of a distinction between offline and online, its leaders must learn to do ministry in virtual, in addition to physical, spaces. The ubiquity of hybrid engagement in digital culture presents three specific challenges for the church leader: to form new ties, to strengthen relationships by augmenting face-to-face bonds with virtual encounters, and to see the whole person.

For reflection and discussion

- To what extent has our community focused outreach efforts primarily on face-to-face encounters like worship attendance?
- Why do you think some church leaders believe face-to-face connections are more important than virtual connections?
- Do *you* agree that face-to-face and online connections are equally important to the digital-age church? Why or why not?

Making hybrid connections: ideas for church leadership	
High-tech	Join several tech companies in promoting Work from Home one day a week, such as a Wednesday. All meetings, from staff gatherings to committee discussions, are held virtually using apps like Zoom and Google docs.
Low-tech	Go paperless in church administration. Eliminate binders, handouts, and other resource-intensive printouts, replacing them with collaborative digital files like Google Docs.
No-tech	Encourage church leaders to distribute, read, and reflect on the subject matter ahead of a meeting. Use the meeting time for thoughtful conversation about people's independent reflection.

5

Redefining Offline Connection

Being church in a tech-shaped culture means connecting online and offline, recognizing that face-to-face community and virtual connection mutually strengthen one another. The Christian communities of a tech-shaped culture are formed from both face-to-face gatherings and the sort of online connections people experience in nearly every other aspect of their lives. The question facing the church leaders in a tech-shaped culture is, how do we build these hybrid connections? Forming these new ties requires more creativity than one might think. With plenty of online businesses and organizations attempting to build followings in cyberspace, the web has become saturated with connection attempts. Being a connective church takes more than an active social media account. It requires a posture of humility, empathy, and consistency. The church of the digital age requires church leaders who will direct energy and creativity not just to online encounters, but to the offline connections that precede digital relationships.

Connecting through ranting

At the University of Nebraska–Lincoln, a Lutheran pastor sits each week in the geographic center of campus next to a sign boldly emblazoned with the neon-lettered words "Rant to me about religion—I'll listen." A typical Thursday at his "rant to me" vigil was recently covered by campus newspaper *The Daily Nebraskan*:

> Within minutes, students sat down and asked [Pastor] White questions about everything—from general advice about their own personal lives to specific questions about religious figures like John Calvin. White has returned to that spot almost every Thursday for the past six years to listen to students.[1]

"I'm out there with that sign every Thursday that the weather permits, from one to three p.m.," says Pastor White, campus pastor at the University of Nebraska–Lincoln since 2011. "It's all about making the church available for pastoral care in a public space."[2]

The "rant to me" ministry started with a commitment to presence and constancy, along with a need to protest. "Early in my tenure, I saw a lot of street preachers," says White.

> They'd say terrible things to students. One day I'm walking, and a street preacher is standing on a corner, yelling at a group of Muslim women. The street preacher had singled them out because of their hijabs. I thought to myself, this university has quite a few international students. If I'm an international student, and I come to the University of Nebraska, and the first thing I see on campus is this guy—that's also the first impression I have of American Christianity.

So Pastor White began his "rant to me" ministry.

Street preachers come in, they are there, then they are gone. They don't stay for long. So I thought, what would it look like if there was a compassionate Christian presence, occupying that same public space, and they're there every week? Then, what would it look like if the dynamics were turned upside down, where the preacher became the listener, and the student became the speaker?

One day, a Muslim student approached Pastor White's table.

He came up to me and asked me about my beliefs. I told him that as a Christian pastor, I preach the Gospel of Jesus Christ. He responded that he too follows the Gospel of Jesus—even as a Muslim. He went on to share his personal story about Jesus. We were sitting out there for an hour and a half, a Muslim student and a Lutheran pastor, talking about what it means to follow Jesus.

"Rant to me about religion" is one aspect of Lutheran Campus Ministry at Nebraska, a dynamic and innovative ministry that forms new ties not through flashy digital tactics, but through a commitment to constant and meaningful connection. White goes on:

At this ministry, searching is a core spiritual practice. We realize that college students are asking the big questions about ultimate things. This phenomenon of America's religious Nones that you sometimes read about is driven by spiritual curiosity—it's not a lack of curiosity. It's dissatisfaction in the ways that the Word has been preached, the way that questions have been suppressed. Campus ministry is about searching for ultimacy and meaning outside the boxes that we've been presented with. We're here to provide a space where you can safely ask questions and talk about the big questions of our spiritual lives.

Adam White's "rant to me" ministry creatively illustrates what it could look like to find new ways to connect in the digital age. His ministry makes the church available to those who would never consider entering a sanctuary on Sunday morning. Pastor White regularly meets his community wherever they are in their search, in a setting that is familiar, comfortable, and open. There are no forms to fill out, no attempts at recruiting new members for a church—just open, raw, and unfiltered conversation about religion, faith, and God. Often, those conversations lead to deeper engagement in the Word and Sacrament. Nebraska's campus ministry offers daily worship services. But the connections, growing out of authentic questions and deep listening, come first. Hybrid connection begin with the willingness to engage the search, whenever, wherever, and however the search happens.

Connecting with a church on wheels

Food facilitates the formation of new ties, and Madison, Wisconsin, is known for its food culture. Specifically, it's known for its food carts, nearly fifty of which daily serve their cuisine to-go. Madison's carts offer a cosmopolitan and colorful array of world cuisine: tacos and empanadas, stir-fry and macaroni and cheese, egg sandwiches and egg rolls. In two locations, one on the University of Wisconsin–Madison Library Mall, the other on the sidewalks of the Capitol Square, a person can eat their way around the world—no ticket to Epcot necessary. In the years I've spent in Madison as a student and a technology professional, I've steadily expanded both my culinary horizons and my waistline. It turns out that Madison's housing market is not the only drain on one's checkbook: regular food cart lunches can empty your bank account faster than you can say "hibachi chicken with pot stickers."

The challenge of the food cart scene in Madison is that it tends to assemble in affluent pockets of the city, saturating the sidewalks of the state capitol and university with delectable fare. Financially secure working professionals and students with their parents' credit cards can eat all the chicken shawarma with falafel they like. But those who live in underserved communities on Madison's southwest side find themselves in food deserts, neighborhoods without access to fresh food aside from what little might be available at gas stations. While I have noticed the occasional hotdog stand and snow cone hut as I have driven home from work, I lament that my access to Madison's food cart scene appears to be another indicator of privilege in this rapidly growing, highly progressive city.

The congregation where my wife and I are members, Good Shepherd Lutheran Church, is surrounded by two economically and racially diverse neighborhoods that are largely food deserts. Of the school-aged students in the community, 75.6 percent are considered "economically disadvantaged." Of the residents, 46.5 percent are people of color.[3] By contrast, Good Shepherd Lutheran is fairly racially and economically homogeneous: most families are relatively affluent; a sizeable majority of the attendees on a given Sunday are white. Still, the neighborhood and the church share a common call and commitment to serve the surrounding community, and Good Shepherd's "Church on Wheels" (CoW) is helping to make that happen.

In an effort to form new ties with its neighbors, Good Shepherd recently opened a food cart ministry. The CoW food cart is adorned with a cartoon cow. The cart mascot wears a glowing halo, integrating Wisconsin's dairy heritage with the levity of a shared outdoor meal on a sun-splashed August afternoon. The CoW maneuvers its way around the neighborhoods of Madison's southwest side, serving everything from homemade lunches and dinners to ice cream sandwiches and sundaes to kids, parents, neighbors, police officers, basketball players, and bicyclists. The CoW staff hands out food to church members and those who have never been to church, the religious and secular alike, all free of charge, no strings attached. It brings candy to trick-or-treaters at Halloween, distributes Easter eggs at the church's annual neighborhood hunt, and hands out ice cream on the first day of Sunday school.

The food is obviously important to the church on wheels, but the Holy CoW is fundamentally about forming new ties through constant and meaningful connection. When Pastor Joe Brosius hitches the food cart to a similarly decorated Honda Pilot, it is not so that the church can go out into the neighborhood to preach or lecture but so that the church can listen. As a church, Good Shepherd seeks to listen intently to their neighbors' perspectives on life in the community. Those who serve food from the cart want to hear whatever the neighbors are interested in sharing, whether they want to chat about which restaurants serve the best BBQ, or which night kids should go trick or treating, or why local housing is becoming unaffordable. All have experiences that the church can learn from. Some may have needs that the church can help to address, but all have a story that a church seeking to form new ties with its surrounding community needs to hear. The CoW provides an inviting space for neighbors to tell their stories on their own terms so that church and community can connect meaningfully, without expectations for what that connection ought to look like.

As a "synodically authorized vehicle," an official church start-up, the CoW is approved for hosting a Service of Word and Sacrament and thus bringing communion out into the city. By combining worshipping on the go with table fellowship, this innovative ministry creates connections based on mutuality. Pastor Joe Brosius explains:

> Worship happens after the meal is served, and is open to anyone. We certainly don't require those who were fed to stay, but we make sure they feel welcomed and included. We bring some scripture, often a passage about biblical love or just society, we sing a song or two, and we have an open forum for prayer and conversation. With the CoW, we seek

to share that God's Word is liberating—not condemning. We seek to share that the church is here to listen. We want to redefine what the church is all about and reclaim the narrative about American Christianity.[4]

"Long-term, we'd like to have the cart in the neighborhood every day, and we'd like to develop a deeper understanding of the needs of the community," says Brosius. "The Church on Wheels is about understanding how all of us, together, can be a factor in meeting the needs of the neighborhood. We're asking ourselves how we can turn our church campus into a community support center—one that exists for collaboration in response to God's call. God's Word changes us all. Together, we want to connect for the sake of justice."

The CoW is one of the ways that church and neighborhood alike discern that call, together, and identify points of connection, not so that the church's pews can fill up on Sunday mornings, but so God's work can be done together by the many hands of southwestern Madison. In a time when emerging leaders in the Evangelical Lutheran Church in America are challenging the church to be more inclusive and committed to justice, this food cart is a strong starting point, particularly for a digital age. The food cart's wheels provide its mobility. The conversations that take place over an ice cream cone or macaroni and cheese provide opportunities for connection. Holy CoW is effective ministry for the digital age, bringing neighborhoods together to be fed with earthly and heavenly food.

Connecting with ashes, on the go

Forming new ties requires a consistent effort to be where the community is gathered. During my years at Google's Ann Arbor office, I didn't always have the time to make it to Ash Wednesday services. This was less about time and more about being a twenty-three-year-old who would rather be at happy hour with coworkers. But every year, I still managed to receive the imposition of ashes. I still heard that reminder that I am dust, and to dust I shall return—that beautiful and haunting rejoinder that annually conjures up within me existential questions and thoughts of necessary change.

Every year on Ash Wednesday, the campus pastors and priests from the University of Michigan's Lutheran and Episcopal ministries would gather at the "Diag," short for the "Diagonal", the University's central pedestrian mall. The Diag is your quintessential campus quad, tilted just enough and intersected with enough sidewalks to make it appear slanted. It's as collegial a setting as one is likely to find on an American campus. Enclosed by stately brick buildings and formidable stone halls of knowledge, it is a prime stopping point for the campus tour, the rare setting on an upper Midwest campus that remains photogenic in all seasons. A gaudy, gold block M lies conspicuously in the center, bringing pride to generations of Michigan alumni, while drawing the ire, and the occasional vandalism, of many students from rival Michigan State University. It's a setting that inspires such reverence among the Maize and Blue faithful that it's not unusual to find battalions of fraternity brothers, who, having nothing better to do, spend the odd all-nighter standing guard at the Diag, protecting the M from wily Spartans and marauding Buckeyes.

In such a populated setting, it is especially noteworthy to see campus clergy in full clerical garb, standing by on a Michigan winter's afternoon, ready to smudge the foreheads of willing passersby. But there they are, every year on Ash Wednesday. Each year on that day, I would stroll out of my office mid-afternoon, meet the campus ministers, chat for a few minutes, and receive the ashes. Such experiences always included brief conversations with the clergy. They would ask how my day was going, inquire about how I kept myself busy, or ask what it was like to work for Google. There were no brazen attempts to preach at me, no bait-and-switch attempts at signing me up for a mailing list. Just clergy, standing on a college campus, assisting in ritual, willing to talk, eager to listen, ready to connect.

Each year, I felt that the ritual added deeply to my journey through the Lenten season. It was a spiritually thought-provoking event, even though it took just fifteen minutes to stand up from my desk, walk to the Diag, receive the imposition of ashes, and return back to my office. Serving as a minor disruptor to the daily grind, the experience helped me to think about what other minor disruptors my spiritual life needed. What were those things that could use letting go of, for Lent and throughout the duration of my search? What was getting in the way—of God, of connection, of living a life of accessibility and responsiveness? Ashes on the Diag is effective ministry for a digital age, fueled by connection, powered by consistent presence. It was, and is, spiritual sustenance for those searching for God with Google.

Conversation starters for forming new ties

Given the content saturation of our online ecosystem, forming new ties in hybrid culture begins offline. Church leaders should begin with an understanding of where their surrounding communities gather together. Those communities might be circled around a food truck or gathered on a college campus quad. Christian ministries that want to serve alongside these communities must establish a consistent, relational, and hospitable presence in these spaces.

Leaders might find value in using a mapping tool like Google Maps to identify the three most important shared spaces in their neighborhoods. Many of these locations are "third spaces," open and welcoming environments between the home and the office. Maybe that location is a coffee shop; perhaps it is a sports stadium or a public park. Find that third space and commit to being there on a consistent basis. Circle that space on a map and place a printout of that map in an area visible to church leaders, like a conference room or office. The map provides a visible reminder that digital age connections between church and community put the church on the go. The map reminds church leaders to commit to being not just in their own space, but in these sacred third spaces, at a repeatable date and time, when the wider community is likely to be gathered.

Church leaders will likely encounter two challenges with forming new ties in these third spaces. The first is the discomfort that comes with venturing outside the church walls. It's not easy to represent the church beyond the building, especially in a secular age. Those who might be apprehensive about this type of outreach would do well to remember that "Christianity" is already represented, although perhaps poorly, in these spaces. It's represented by data on declining church attendance. It's represented by news reports on the ethical failures and financial impropriety of those in church leadership. The unsavory side of the tradition is already out in the world, and we need to be there, too.

The second challenge is the tendency to pivot too quickly towards churchiness. When leaders head out into the community, their first priority must be to listen. Prayer is not a priority in these contexts, though it should be available upon request. Nor is preaching. These moments are exclusively about forming connections in whatever form that takes. Forming new ties is a prerequisite, both to engaging the big questions of faith and to building a church community online.

When I was in high school, the adult leaders of the area Young-Life ministry gathered in the school commons for lunch for one hour every Tuesday. There was no attempt to proselytize, preach, or promote any programs. There was just conversation, listening, and relationship building. They often brought chocolate. They always brought a great smile and a receptive ear. I would join them regularly, as would many of the students at West High School. The leaders didn't have an agenda—they just wanted to hear how we were doing. We talked about sports, we talked about classes, we talked about what it was like to grow up in Appleton. I still consider those leaders in Appleton's YoungLife program to be among the most influential voices in my faith development, not only for the example they set as Christian leaders, committed to service and care for their community, but for their consistency. They formed new ties in that high school community that remain fifteen years later, simply because they showed up and listened.

For reflection and discussion

- With whom does the ministry seek to serve? What exactly is its community?
- Where are the third spaces in which members of this community gather?
- How could the ministry be consistently available within these spaces?
- What are the attitudes or perceptions that those gathered in these third spaces have towards the church?
- What would it look like to extend a consistent presence in these physical spaces with digital technology?

Making hybrid connections: ideas for faith formation and Christian education	
High-tech	Create an app offering daily contemplative experiences with the readings your congregation will engage together on Sunday. Upload recordings of a church leader reading a text, perhaps several times a day in the style of Lectio Divina. Conclude with a recorded prayer. Utilize push notifications to encourage app downloaders to use the app regularly.
Low-tech	Use social media to share curated digital resources related to a Sunday's readings or sermon themes. For example, you might use a church Facebook page during Holy Week to share videos about the Temple, Passover feasts, and the Roman justice system.
No-tech	Use the "flipped classroom" methodology in your Christian education programming. Share any lecture-based, informational content ahead of a class meetup, and use the time together not to present anything new but to discuss how to respond or to apply the subject matter in one's faith life.

6

Integrating
Online Connection

When church leaders are forming new ties in face-to-face communities, a parallel step is to integrate the virtual and physical aspects of our tech-shaped culture. Churches tend to be less effective and efficient at creating connections in virtual contexts than they are in physical contexts. But connection in a digital age demands both in-person meetups and online conversations; it requires meaningful encounters both face-to-face and through connective technologies like Zoom and Slack. Forming new ties will involve significant integration of the virtual in contexts that have long involved only face-to-face encounters, such as worship, leadership, and sabbath keeping and other spiritual practices. Integrating the virtual is not about discarding the richness of the church's tradition of face-to-face community. Integrating the virtual is about augmenting what is great about local forms of connection with the constant reach and meaningful relationality of our online experiences.

"My phone facilitates mobile connection, but I still have a grounded sense of place in the church where people have been around since the 1750s," says Keith Anderson, author of *Click2Save* and *The Digital*

Cathedral. "We should keep being in this one place, while recognizing the need to join together through wide virtual connection."[1]

Virtual integration in the workplace

In 2016, my wife, Annie, and I moved back to Wisconsin. I took a job with Zendesk, at the time a relatively small but rapidly growing contributor to the tech scene. I joined Zendesk to start a learning and development team—a team focused on establishing a culture of skill and leadership development in a startup environment. While Zendesk may not carry the brand recognition of Google, I was intrigued by their mission of enhancing customer relationships through intuitive software. How many of us have had the experience of requesting customer support or buying from someone completely clueless about our situation? That's the problem Zendesk seeks to solve through its clever synthesis of powerful tech, trendy Danish design, and easy customer experiences.

The similarity between Google's and Zendesk's missions and cultures made my career transition significantly easier than I anticipated. Both companies provide after-work outdoor yoga classes, fully stocked refrigerators with a prismatic selection of La Croix, and free lunches to workers (because they are bought-in to the idea that the best workplace conversations happen over a shared meal). More significantly, both companies invest in employees, value collaboration, and go out of their way to facilitate connection. They're the sort of firms where CEOs stay late to answer employee questions over happy-hour beverages and where team volunteering events happen regularly, even during the workday.

Zendesk, like many global businesses, runs on collective, virtual connections. I've learned the strength of these connections as I've collaborated with colleagues who seldom gather in the same location. Many software companies split their teams among several far-flung time zones. At Google, several of my counterparts were located in Hyderabad in southern India. At Zendesk, much of my team is based in Manila. While this creates challenges any time an important meeting is called for, it allows for around-the-clock development and productivity. I've worked with technology companies with as few as five and as many as fifty-thousand employees that take this handoff-based approach to design and development. Together, we've launched advertising campaigns, published training courses, written how-to guides, and recorded company podcasts. As it turns out, we need not all be in the same place to connect effectively!

Today, my team has employees working on three continents, with offices in Madison, Dublin, and Manila. I've often been impressed not just with our productivity, but by the strength of our relationships. Using little more than Google Docs, Calendar, and Zoom, our globally distributed team designed, built, and implemented an employee onboarding program. Then we implemented e-learning to help learners build their skillsets on their own schedule in their preferred learning contexts. Next, we published an extensive catalog of on-demand professional skills courses. All of this we completed without setting foot in the same conference room. While we did eventually meet as a team (international visitors love Wisconsin in early January!), we came together digitally to launch a culture of learning—powered by virtual connection, creativity, trust, and sparkling water!

Learning to integrate the virtual at church

I know firsthand, mostly as a consequence of my spending too much time on committees, the church's ambivalence towards digital forms of togetherness. Since I was confirmed, I've volunteered for committees on marketing, boards of directors for camps and congregations, task forces for leadership development, and planning groups for liturgical seasons. I've written podcast scripts with communications committees, designed new web pages with digital "transformation" task forces, and drafted new mission statements with church councils. The prospect of no longer needing to travel to committee meetings may well have been an unconscious motivation for writing this book!

All of this committee work was done in face-to-face meetings, many of which required driving long distances, zipping (or crawling) through traffic, or endlessly circling the block in the vain search for a downtown parking spot in Ann Arbor or Madison. Much of this work could have been just as easily completed by connecting virtually—via phone call, web conference, or simply by email. It's been my experience that merely mentioning some form of digital togetherness in a church committee setting triggers a swell of apprehension. The prevailing sentiment is anxiety over whether any truly meaningful work can be accomplished without battling traffic, snagging a parking spot, and meeting a team for the one twenty-minute span that works for just over half the group—all of this to do work that could easily have been completed with just one or two emails or a phone or web conference. While it is true that dropped calls, poor audio quality, and patchy video feeds can create frustration, such concerns should be viewed in light of the advantages—the accessibility, affordability, and efficiency—of digital connection.

As virtual connection shapes administration and leadership, it will continue to change the way we gather for worship. Many leaders are beginning to recognize that while worship is a deeply embodied experience, it need not be done in a face-to-face environment. Efforts to open a congregation's worship to those outside of the four walls of the building will continue to grow in importance.

Live streaming worship will continue to be a free and easy method for facilitating connection across a distributed community. All it takes is a Facebook page, a smartphone, and a hand or stand to hold the smartphone. Live streaming offers a viable solution to help churches bring the Word to those who are unable to attend on a given Sunday, while building bridges to the differently abled within a faith community, those who may be physically or mentally unable to leave their homes, travel to church, and enter the sanctuary. It helps churches to connect to what Heidi Campbell describes as the "multisite reality" of the digital age church, the blurring of boundaries between physical and digital spaces.[2]

"One of the most significant recent digital trends is that the offline experience is no longer the ultimate grounding of reality," says Dr. Campbell. "Even offline connection is much more dispersed and disconnected than it once was."

Even in a tech-shaped culture, the church is still a community formed by Word and Sacrament. With recent advances in the video and audio recording capabilities of our phones and the accessibility of streaming platforms like Facebook Live, it is essential for church leaders to continue to welcome to welcome worshippers in digital spaces. When your community gathers for a public worship service, it should be live-streamed. Preaching should be broadcast live, then posted to social media for later viewing. Prayers of the people should gather up the petitions of those in attendance both physically and virtually. On occasion, readings should be provided by those outside the physical sanctuary. While the communal experience of singing may not transfer to a web group, words, lyrics, or interpretations of a piece of music should be provided for the reflection of those assembled online. Christian communities also need to experiment with services held entirely in virtual contexts, where all congregants and leaders gather from their own location using tools like Zoom and YouTube, both of which afford low-cost and easily usable web conferencing tools that are widely used for public worship. The service is fundamentally about God serving those who have gathered together. To not stream the worship service is to block those on the other side of the screen from having that encounter with the grace of God.

Live streaming is a necessary and widely adopted first step towards virtual integration in the church, though church leaders will need to be thoughtful about creating parity in the offline and online worship experience. As more churches stream worship and other gatherings, leaders should think creatively about building a bridge between virtual and face-to-face experiences, lest virtual worship feel like a second-tier experience. One ministry, the VR Church, where pastors and parishioners alike use virtual reality headsets to join together in an immersive, digital environment, is the first-ever Christian worshipping community to gather entirely in virtual reality. On a mission "to explore and communicate God's love through virtual reality, augmented reality, and next generation technologies," VR Church brings together an online community of Christians, atheists, preachers, parishioners, believers, and skeptics for weekly worship, daily prayer, and constant conversation.[3]

Anyone with a virtual reality headset is welcome at VR Church: power on the headset, open up the app, and join the conversation. While virtual reality headsets are hardly as ubiquitous as smartphones and laptops, sales of these units are expected to grow at over fifty-six percent through 2021, at which point the industry expects to sell over eighty-two million units annually.[4] Even though VR Church is built upon an emergent technology, it is defined more by its unconditional welcome and expansive sense of community. "Everyone is invited to VR Church. It doesn't matter if you believe in God or not," reads their homepage.[5]

The ministry has three digitally integrated practices: Sunday worship, life group, and online discussion. "VR Church is built on this idea that the church is a community, not a one-hour event on Sunday," says Pastor DJ Soto, founder of VR Church. "We gather for worship in virtual reality on Sunday, then throughout the week, we gather for life groups. When we're not all in VR, hundreds of us join in conversation on the Discord social media platform, bringing our questions and conversations wherever we go."[6]

According to Pastor Soto, some in the VR Church engage with Christian spiritual practice exclusively through virtual reality. Some have never walked into a physical church building. Some have been ostracized and kicked out of a church. All find the discussions, the teachings, and the community of a church in VR to be authentic, inclusive, and engaging. Says Pastor Soto:

> We are truly an inclusive community. We even have quite a few atheists and agnostics who join us every week. They're curious about spirituality. Many of them were raised in the church, and the church is part of their identity. The virtual reality experience and the anonymity of the avatar allows them to be fully present, in a non-judgmental conversation.

VR Church is a virtually integrated worshipping community that facilitates authenticity. As Pastor Soto indicated in our conversation, many attendees feel more comfortable worshipping through a virtual reality avatar (a digital, image-based representation of oneself for use in VR) than in a face-to-face church. The anonymity of the avatar allows the attendee to drop what they view as the "performative" aspects of church attendance. Freed from the implicit need to conform to the standards of a physical worshipping community, attendees at VR Church worship together, virtually and authentically.

Not every ministry needs to be as digitally immersive as the VR Church. Not every church needs to hold its committee meetings via web conference, and not every congregation needs to live stream its worship services, though each of these could be effective in facilitating connection and togetherness in virtual environments. But in this hybrid cultural landscape, where offline and online connection are often viewed with equal regard, every church leader needs a strategy for connecting with a culture deeply embedded in digital experiences. Every church leader needs a plan for integrating a hybrid nature for the sake of ministry.

Integrating virtual technology with spiritual practice

One of the strengths of the Christian tradition is the ease with which community gatherings, worship in particular, inspire and support individual practice. The benediction and sending at the conclusion of the liturgy facilitate this transfer, commissioning those assembled to go forth, to contemplate and act, to pray and to serve wherever one goes. A challenge for the church leader in a culture of hybrid connections is to facilitate spiritual practice with technology, to coach those gathered to practice their faith with digital tools.

In Christianity, spiritual practice invites the integration of collective, networked faith into each person's daily life. While spiritual practice doesn't require digital technology, our virtual technology makes it possible to integrate spiritual disciplines with other daily habits. Digitally integrated spiritual practice is the experience of God in prayer, meditation, yoga, music, and other arts—through podcasts and blog posts, digital videos and social media communities, chat threads and e-devotionals—and are all highly accessible in the moment. Digitally integrated spiritual practice is online affirmation; it is digital lament. Including praise and thanksgiving, blessing and celebration, it is as authentic a church as any. It's software and sermon; it's spiritual conversation on social media. It is, broadly speaking, whatever inspires us to ask life's biggest questions. When we think about what it means for the church to create connections in a digital age, we must continue to consider what it means to connect people not only to institutions or even to other people, but to spiritual practices.

When I was in seminary, a classmate joked that it wouldn't be long before professionalized clergy were replaced with self-employed clerical contractors using "Uber for Pastors." In this hypothetical app, you could indicate you needed a baptism, a first communion, a confession, or a sermon, and the nearest priest or pastor from your preferred denomination would be at your door in minutes. You could arrange a wedding ceremony without the strain of premarital counseling. You could be confirmed without driving to church every Wednesday evening for three years. You could turn to Uber Eats for your takeout dinner, then flip back to Uber for Pastors for your bread and wine. Just to be clear, Uber for Pastors was just a joke, it is not an actual app. It's not a great illustration of the virtually integrated church, as it precludes the involvement of community. Still, it illustrates how the future of spiritual practice will involve customizable digital technology deployed to support an individual in their search for God.

Church leaders have an important role in facilitating these spiritual practices. There are two specific pastoral responsibilities related to virtual spiritual practice: curation and creation. Both curating and creating content involve partnering with members of the community to introduce, model, and promote virtually integrated habits for spiritual practice.

Curation involves the careful selection of resources. Today's church leader should think of themselves as a digital librarian, developing an awareness of digital tools supporting prayer, scripture reading, contemplation, and service. Ministers should be discerning users of religious apps, blogs, podcasts, and websites that can extend the shared work of the people to the practice of the individual. The church leader first needs to know the mission of the community, to understand the needs of its individuals, and to locate and share the most relevant resources. A leader of a community who is focused on nurturing a community called to work for economic and social justice might curate scriptural content about God's compassion for the poor. A leader of a community called to political advocacy on behalf of migrants and refugees might curate and compile contemplation apps to ground the difficult work in God's presence. Similarly, a leader of a community called to minister to families might curate short Christian podcasts, accessible to all ages, that the family can listen to while in the car together. There are ample digital resources available for spiritual practice, some focused on prayer, some focused on scripture, others focused on contemplation, reflection, yoga, and many more. The task of the pastor as curator is to evaluate resources' quality and relevance, and to share them with the community.

Content creation involves the assembly of websites, blog posts, podcast episodes, and other types that will resonate within the community. The call to digital content creation is a call to discern what cannot simply be curated but must instead be invented. The process of creating content for spiritual practice is surprisingly easy with ubiquitous technology. An iPhone provides all the tools one needs to produce a basic podcast or video series. A new Google Doc or a Blogger account provides the blank canvas for writing. The barrier to entry as a content creator is low. It just requires the will to be inventive, the awareness of the needs of the community, and a commitment to strengthening connections. Where I live, in politically and religiously progressive Madison, website content that helps community members to study the narrative arcs of various books of the Bible might not be as engaging as blog content that magnifies how these books lead us towards compassion for the refugee and concern for the immigrant—and how members of that community could live out that calling in their city. Each context is different, and the content ministers create must reflect the uniqueness of that context.

Digitally integrated spiritual practice is not about the abandonment of collective gatherings or liturgy. It should not replace Bible studies, retreats, service projects, or even committee meetings. It shouldn't supplant pastoral visits, hospital chaplaincy, or after-church coffee hours.

Rather, it is about the extension of this work to the individual with the help of digital tools. The experience of God's gracious actions in a community must continue to work after the community has been sent out after worship. God works in our lives even when we are by ourselves, alone with our thoughts with a few quiet moments to breathe deeply and to be with God.

A personal Sabbath

Regardless of context, all Christian communities can and should support Sabbath rest. Paradoxically, while religion needs to focus on plugging in to the digital age, it also needs to minister to those who struggle to unplug, to provide experiences of Sabbath rest to those navigating perpetual virtual connection. The demands of constant virtual connectivity in our tech-shaped culture have created an unmet need for rest and disconnection. If the church is to facilitate hybrid connection, it should also consider the necessity of occasional disconnection from virtual environments.

We are living our virtually addicted lives at an unsustainable and harried pace. According to *The Nation*, thirty-three percent of Americans work over forty-five hours each week, and 9.7 million of us work over sixty hours from Monday through Friday.[7] Full-time US workers spend an average of forty-seven hours per week on the job—and these numbers are steadily, insidiously increasing.[8] Meanwhile, commutes are slowly getting longer, demands on students' time are exponentially increasing, and what little time we once had available for activities like church is rapidly fading.[9] The United States Bureau of Labor Statistics found that the average American now spends under twenty minutes per day on all "organizational, civic, and religious activities." That figure, which includes data from retirees and part-time workers, is likely a vast overrepresentation of what little time we actually spend on religious practice. Unsurprisingly, these digital demands are beginning to adversely affect our health. According to the United Nations' 2019 report, "Safety and Health at the Heart of the Future of Work," our culture of obsessive virtual availability to our work can even be fatal, contributing to up to 2.8 million premature deaths each year.[10]

We need Sabbath more than ever. We need to experience Sabbath rest in community, and we need a Sabbath practice that is culturally feasible and virtually accessible. But what exactly is Sabbath in tech-shaped culture? At its most basic level, Sabbath is the practice of time away from work. This could be as expansive as an entire day of the week, though it need not be confined to Sundays. To Andreas Schuele, the most ancient origins of the word *sabbath* did not connote the seventh day of the week or even a full day of rest. "While the Sabbath eventually became a weekly holiday, characterized as a day of rest, this may not have been its original function," writes Schuele in the *New Interpreter's Dictionary of the Bible*.[11] The practice of Sabbath can simply be an intentional pause: a morning without email, a full hour for lunch and a walk, an evening away from the internet.

"Stemming from the Genesis narrative in which God rests after the work of creation and specifically blesses a day for humans to do the same, Sabbath reminds us that being human is more than just work," says Christin Tomy of the *National Catholic Reporter*. "Sabbath isn't about rules, but about restoring relationships . . . Sabbath reminds us who we are and whose we are . . . We practice Sabbath not just for ourselves, but for the whole world."[12]

Sabbath keeping has always been a radical act, empowered by religious communities in opposition to prevailing social and economic forces. The Sabbath concept in ancient Judaism had no parallel anywhere in the ancient Near East. It was an innovation, a disruption of the daily grind.[13] Especially today, the claim that our existence is about more than achievement and connection is completely and utterly counter-cultural. It is also completely and utterly essential to our well-being. In the midst of the digital age, we all need oases of grace and unconditional acceptance that provide a reprieve from the breakneck pace of virtual connection. We need a place to escape the high expectations and tough accountability of the workplace. We need a space to rest, if only for a few fleeting moments, amid the blinding brightness of our phone's push notifications.

The church has the opportunity to facilitate an experience of Sabbath rest using the same technologies that have at times prevented us from experiencing needed rest. Given our cultural climate, finding a way to facilitate virtual experiences of Sabbath rest may be religion's greatest opportunity and gift to society.

I recently reframed my morning routine as a time for a few moments of virtual sabbath. Just before I get in the car or climb on the bicycle to travel to my office, I spend a few moments in contemplation. I typically start by reading Richard Rohr's daily meditation (from the Center for Action and Contemplation) or Luther Seminary's "God Pause" devotional—both online resources. Next, I spend a few minutes in prayer or meditation, often with the help of the Calm app. As I'm weaving across the bike paths of downtown Madison or stuck in downtown traffic, I may be listening to The Liturgists Podcast or Richard Rohr's podcast, "Another Name for Everything." By the time I arrive at the office, I'm calm, centered, and open to the ways in which God will work through my vocation. These practices were recommended to me by pastors, fellow seminarians, and friends who understood my context and my spiritual interests.

Luther Seminary's God Pause devotional, a daily electronic meditation on a passage from the week's lectionary, is a key part of that practice. Each meditation is 150 words or fewer, including the reading itself, a reflection on the scripture, and a short prayer. "The goal of God Pause has always been to provide a daily spiritual resource focused around the lectionary," says Jim Boyce, professor emeritus at Luther Seminary. "We've published God Pause since 2002. It's always been a collaborative effort with the seminary's alumni. We have approximately fifty-two writers each year, writing for an audience of Christians around the world."[14]

Boyce indicates that God Pause is about connecting with readers wherever they find themselves, for a few moments of faith development during a busy day. "It's about faith formation, relationships, and collaboration," says Boyce. "We want the language to be inclusive. We want it to be relational, and we want it to reach the church at large."

Over fifteen thousand readers subscribe to these daily email meditations, which reflect on readings from the Old Testament, Psalms, New Testament, and the week's hymnody. The meditations can easily be embedded in any app or church website with source code made available by Luther Seminary's web development team.

"When I think back on all of my years at Luther, I am most proud of outreach projects like God Pause," says Boyce. "To be able to look back and say we were able to provide those as a resource for lay and rostered people in the church around the world, and to know that people around the world are finding this meaningful and using this regularly is tremendously rewarding."

Even in the midst of my busiest and most stressful days, God Pause provides an infusion of grounding and grace. When I need a break from the pace of life, I take out my phone and open the day's God Pause email. It's an experience of Sabbath, delivered daily to my inbox.

Leaders in the ministry world must recognize the desperate need for Sabbath in a digital age. As coaches, curators, and creators of content, it is their call not just to preside over a sixty-minute service on the Sabbath day, but to integrate Sabbath practice in the daily experience of their network.

For reflection and discussion

• How can lay leaders, clergy, and staff use digital technology to facilitate virtual connection in the running of the ministry?

• Consider a typical worship service. How could this worship service be extended to those not in the same physical location?

• What types of spiritual disciplines are practiced within this community? What would a digitally integrated expression of these practices look like?

• How might church leaders coach those within the community to adopt a digitally integrated spiritual practice?

• How might you help extend the experience of Sabbath into the daily practice of your network? How might digital tools help?

Making hybrid connections: ideas for worship	
High-tech	Join the wave of churches offering an annual Worship from Home experience, a Sunday where all worshippers join from their own location. Use a webinar-style technology like Zoom or Cisco WebEx to stream everything from readings, prayers, and sermons to songs. Be sure to share the worship leadership responsibilities as you would on any other Sunday!
Low-tech	Live-stream every sermon to Facebook Live. This posts the sermon to the church's Facebook page as it is happening. Record the sermon with a smartphone. (Just be sure to hold it steady!)
No-tech	Select a third space in the community (a coffee shop, a park, a pizzeria) and commit to consistent presence and connection-forming within that space.

7

Connecting with the Whole Person

In a tech-shaped culture, the need for Sabbath rest is clear. Equally important is the need to learn to see the whole person in digital spaces. We are living in a time when many of our interactions take place on digital platforms that are devoid of the nonverbal context provided by face-to-face communication. When we connect online, we read and we post, we consider and we comment. But when others see what we have posted, they don't see the details of our situation; they don't see our body language or hear the tone we intend. When we cannot see the whole person, we can process only words, not the details beyond the screen. Even when we can see photos or videos, which provide more information than printed words alone, we judge images without scrutinizing what's beyond the view of the lens or what is edited and filtered out. We reduce the complexities of a person or group to images and sounds on our phones. Trolling, vitriol, and cyberbullying are often the result. We are living in a time of context collapse, in which others online can reduce our identities into over-simplified distortions. In a social-media-obsessed culture, seeing the whole person is more difficult than ever.

The tools and platforms that are part of digital connectivity began as transactional, and at times anonymized, tools for pithy exchanges.

As messaging apps have evolved, they have become incrementally more personalized. Through sound and image, users have been able to share more of their context in digital connections. Still, challenges abound. When we encounter opinions with which we disagree, our first thought is often to unfriend, unfollow, or to cancel. "Trolling," intentionally inflaming and sowing discord, is everywhere on social media and is often targeted towards people of color, women, and members of the LGBTQIA+ community. Hate speech on digital platforms is not uncommon, even as tech firms roll out policies designed to combat it. Comments left on anonymized communication platforms like Reddit, or the notorious YouTube comments section, are especially disturbing. Cyberbullying is particularly problematic in schools, as technologies like Snapchat render digital communications untraceable.

Given the extent of context collapse in digital communication, perhaps it is impossible to truly see the whole person. But if we acknowledge that our digital perspectives are limited and that we are prone to making judgments that are lacking in empathy and understanding, perhaps we can see another person with clear hearts and minds. Attempting to see the whole person requires a mindset of humility, a mindset that combines the recognition that our digital vantage point is limited and that we must treat one another with grace. Seeing the whole person and treating them as such is the extension of grace into digital spaces that have too frequently been defined by shame.

Communications professor Heidi Campbell has written extensively about religion and new media. She is the author of five books on the subject, which focus on topics as broad as the role of religion in digital games to the methods by which religious communities begin to engage new technologies. I asked her about the next big question for church leaders in the digital age. I wanted to know if it would have to do with a new technology, maybe virtual or augmented reality, or perhaps all of the new internet-connected objects in our homes. But according to Dr.

Campbell, the future of religious engagement with new media is about not just the technology, but the ethics.

"I think there are a lot of ethical issues with technology use that religion needs to engage," says Dr. Campbell. "How do we treat the person on the other side of this screen? What does it mean to be human in hybrid encounters? Who is my neighbor, and how do we treat them in digital contexts?"[1]

Ministry innovators are beginning to engage these questions and explore what it means to see the whole person in digital contexts. One of those innovators is Shamika Goddard, a PhD student and "tech chaplain." A recent graduate of Union Theological Seminary, Shamika regularly found herself assisting students, staff, and faculty with questions related to technology on campus.

"My tech chaplaincy began at the Union IT Department," says Goddard. "As I coached and taught others about the use of digital tools, I started reflecting on what it would look like to combine the practices of chaplaincy and pastoral care within a frame of technology."[2]

I first met Shamika Goddard at a virtual faith-formation event hosted by Virginia Theological Seminary. The event started and ended with virtual worship—a service of the Word, held via Zoom. The service included prayers, readings, responses, and blessings, providing a glimpse at one expression of liturgy in the digital age. Between the opening and closing worship services, participants gathered for online presentations and breakout discussions led by ministry innovators. Goddard hosted a breakout session about Christian advocacy in digital contexts. She commented:

> When someone needs help with something technical, they can feel embarrassed, anxious, or inadequate. Asking for expert help with one's email or website sometimes includes the tacit acknowledgement that I am at my limits—that I

don't know what I'm doing. Many of us have had experiences where someone in tech support has made us feel "less than," where a condescending comment has made us feel stupid. I want to educate and empower people when it comes to technology. I want to bring God's grace into our conversation— to make God's presence available and known, especially in the context of technology.

Goddard consults with nonprofits and ministry organizations, offering a range of services including. Offering a range of services including tech audits, email strategy development, and website design, she coaches, teaches, and supports her clients as they work toward their "digital dreams." According to her website, "Instead of a technician who simply fixes a problem, a Tech Chaplain aims to train and equip faith leaders, organizations, and communities with digital skills. Together, we can decrease fear and anxiety and increase self-confidence and empowerment."[3]

Goddard demonstrates how to navigate hybrid spaces with a mindset of humility and empathy, and to actively seek to extend grace into digital spaces. Goddard's call is to start conversations in churches and in educational communities about bringing grace and compassion into virtual settings by being available to the whole person, not just to their questions about digital tools. She says:

> This is work I feel called to as a person of faith. I'm drawn to 2 Timothy 1:7—that God has not given us a spirit of fear, but of power and of love and of a sound mind. Especially in the church, there's so much anxiety around technology. When I work with someone, I want them to know throughout our exchange that we're both humans. We're both children of God. So, let us work together, with the technology, to learn alongside one another.

But Goddard doesn't stop at providing a people-centered approach to tech support and training. "While in seminary, I was looking through available spirituality apps. There were apps for prayer and contemplation, but I noticed that the sacraments were missing. This important part of the liturgy was not represented in digital form." So Goddard got to work. She and fellow Union seminarian Kenji Kuramitsu wrote, designed, and published a mobile app for digital communion called E-ucharist. There are many reasons why someone may not be able to receive the sacrament in a church: physical or mental disability, a past traumatic experience with the church, or simply finding oneself far from a faith community's gathering. Goddard and Kuramitsu's work boldly attempts to extend the gracious experience of sharing this sacrament.

"We had a lot of prayer and conversation, and we decided to go forward with it. I've really enjoyed the project," says Goddard.

> E-ucharist has art, it has music, it has singing. It brings the sacrament to those who feel the need to receive it but are unable to receive it at a church for many different reasons. The app provides the prayers and the spiritual grounding. You provide the elements of bread and wine, taking communion in a setting that is safe and comfortable for you.

Goddard acknowledges that some in the church have pushed back on the E-ucharist app.

> Some people are not comfortable with a digital eucharistic prayer. They think that the sacrament has to be completely corporeal. But when I read the scriptures, Jesus is remarkably short on detailed instructions for the Lord's Supper. We're commanded to eat and drink—the rest is our own, non-scripturally based tradition.

Ultimately, Goddard hopes that the availability of the Eucharist in a digital format will start a needed conversation. She observes, "Technology is changing so much with faith and spirituality. We need to have dialogue around what it means to make the Lord's Supper more widely available. We need to have dialogue about what it means to see the wholeness of each of us in a digital space." Thanks to Goddard's availability and focus on the whole person, God is a little more visible across hybrid culture.

Seeing the whole person in the congregation

Church leaders may not be able to solve the challenge of context collapse, but they can and should address it. Christian communities have an important role to play if more of us in this tech-shaped culture are to develop the willingness to see the whole person on the other side of the screen. This work must begin with an awareness-raising dialogue. Christian leaders should start facilitating a broad conversation within their congregations on what it means to live in a time of context collapse, in which our interactions with one another are often fragmentary and illusory. As congregations raise awareness of environmental degradation, systemic racism, and economic inequality, they should be educating their communities on context collapse and why it is a problem that Christians are called to address. Within our Christian communities, we should be raising awareness of the limitations of digital communication, not to dissuade people from using these platforms, but to promote a sense of humility among those who do. Part of this conversation involves raising an awareness of the unsavory side of digital communications, particularly trolling, shaming, cyberbullying, and most recently, cancel culture (which can manifest as a form of digital ostracism or exile on social media). Most of this conversation should be focused on what it means to extend the grace of God into digital spaces in a spirit of humility and empathy.

Christian leaders need to be at the forefront of this dialogue for two reasons. The first reason comes from Christian "anthropology," our tradition's understanding of the importance of personhood. We believe people are created, not as incomplete beings, but in the image of God, and that therefore those on both sides of the screen possess dignity and deserve equality. This should be the basis of our common resolve that our personhood matters offline and online, even when the context that defines that personhood is not readily accessible. The second reason is that we share a commitment to extending the grace of God into a world that so desperately needs to experience that grace. God calls us as Christian leaders to be a source of healing in contexts of strife and suffering, the internet included. With the rapid pace of technical change, digital culture hasn't yet reflected on how to make space for grace and healing. It is up to Christian leaders to catalyze that reflection, to establish that space, to help us to live into new ways of connecting.

For reflection and discussion

- What digital tools are most widely used within your community? What challenges do those tools present for viewing the full image of God within one another?
- How could this community start a dialogue about the challenges of seeing the whole person in digital spaces?
- How can we use digital tools for empathy and advocacy?

SECTION 3
COLLABORATION

· ·

As the church of a tech-shaped culture learns to create space for questions and live in hybrid connection, its leaders must simultaneously foster collaboration, the practice of working together toward a shared objective. This will take a consistent, churchwide commitment to working and thinking together not as individuals distributed across a hierarchy, but as co-equal contributors. Collaboration is needed in the church not just because collaboration promotes altruism, but because it's become an expectation of those living in a tech-shaped culture. When church embraces collaboration, everyone in the community becomes more effective at fulfilling their vocation of loving and serving their neighbor.

The cultural value of collaboration stems, in part, from the rapid spread of collaborative digital technologies, software that allows multiple people to work on a project simultaneously. As real-time collaboration software becomes increasingly common at home and in the workplace, we are increasingly able to think together: to brainstorm, to write, to critique, and to revise. Real-time tools, from Google Docs to Zoom, Microsoft Office 365 to Wikipedia, facilitate joint action, inclusive of multiple voices and perspectives, regardless of one's current time or physical location. While this type of software is now quite common, it wasn't long ago that technology connected workers but supported only offline, individual, and asynchronous work.

Collaborative technology and the cultural value of collaboration have become increasingly widespread for several reasons. First, collaboration facilitates inclusivity. As technology becomes increasingly collaborative, work itself becomes decreasingly individualistic. We become more adept at incorporating diverse perspectives from across the group, demonstrating respect for each person in the process. Collaboration also fosters learning. Collaborative technology allows communities to develop knowledge, skills, and attitudes through the creative construction of shared experiences and the asking of shared questions. In this way, groups that collaborate can be more efficient, even more effective than individuals.

Christian communities should embrace the cultural value of collaboration for many of the same reasons that it has been embraced by the broader culture. When we in the church collaborate, we ensure perspectives are more well-rounded and inclusive. We mitigate individual biases and create opportunities for the broader community to grow in faith through experiential learning. Through collaboration, we develop a clearer sense of God's work in our community and how we are called to participate in service to the neighbor. When we collaborate, we become increasingly aware that we are the messengers through which God's story unfolds. We become increasingly mindful of the fact that our lives are the conduits by which the grace of God extends into the world. With this strengthened awareness, we come to understand that we don't simply "go to" church. We are the church, called together to be part of God's mission in service to the world for the reconciliation and healing of all things.

8

Learning
and Leading
Collaboratively

I have experienced the importance of collaboration and collaborative tech while working for businesses that build real-time tools, the most widely known of which is Google Docs. Launched in 2006, Google's suite of real-time collaboration tools has come to include a word processing application (Docs), a spreadsheet program (Sheets), and a presentation tool (Slides). Any file created using one of these applications is conveniently stored for free in the cloud-based Google Drive.

Before Google Docs, collaboration and peer editing were slow, often tedious, and offline tasks, involving unending email volleys and a dizzying reel of document versions. As a college student in the pre-Google Docs era, I remember spending late nights in the library untangling the six versions of a group project stored on six different laptops, in a futile effort to identify the highest quality copy for submission. Collaboration was something we did, begrudgingly, knowing it was required for a passing grade. Just as the technological graveyards of the pre-laptop era are filled with typewriter correction fluids like Liquid

Paper, the technological graveyards of my college years are filled with version after version of group term papers.

But today, collaboration is no longer a burden, at least not practically speaking. Anyone with an internet connection and access to Google Docs can simultaneously add comments and action items, ask questions, offer feedback, and decide on next steps. Writers can edit a manuscript from anywhere with an internet connection. Analysts can forecast budgets from offices on opposite sides of the world. Professional speakers can solicit suggestions on their slides before going on stage at a conference. And first-time authors like me can easily list, view, and fix their myriad grammatical mistakes on the go with a few taps of the thumb—all at no cost to creators and collaborators.

While Microsoft Office, an offline, largely non-collaborative technology, remains the dominant player in business productivity software, Google's market share is starting to catch up. From 2015 to 2017, the number of businesses using Google Docs for real-time collaboration increased from two million to four million.[1] Every day, over 800 million users view, edit, or share a Google Doc.[2] The ability to collaborate in real-time will continue to erode market share of non-cloud-based business tools—and Google Docs, once the pipe dream of engineers working on a search engine, may one day become as dominant as Gmail or Search.

Like Search and Gmail, Google Docs promoted a new standard within software development. Catalyzed by the exponential growth of cloud computing, the fastest-growing business software firms, from Salesforce to Slack, from HubSpot to Zendesk, build tools that centralize real-time collaboration across a network. The software industry has shifted from offering collaboration tools as an "add-on" or "feature" to creating and supporting collaborative experiences as a core expectation.

The collaborative architecture of software is visible in two of Google Docs' most innovative and important features: comments mode and suggestions mode. With comments, you can provide your reaction to my work, and I can provide my reaction to your work. Hopefully, these reactions are welcomed, listened to, and appreciated. With suggestions, I can provide real-time constructive guidance on document structure, word choice, slide layout, formula usage, and anything else that might be reasonably done with a Google Doc. The comments and suggestions modes facilitate real-time feedback that help us align our work to the needs of an audience. While writing this book, I looked back on the number of comments made on my projects over one calendar year. As best as I could tell, there were over 650 unique suggestions, likely thousands more if I were to factor in replies stemming from a suggestion. The vast majority of these suggestions resulted in higher quality work synthesized from many diverse perspectives.

Zendesk, my current vocational home, provides collaborative software for customer conversations. In a digital age, businesses need to speak, message, chat, email, and talk to their clients while maintaining a coherent understanding of customer needs. Zendesk provides a platform on which to build relationships through these means. As a company, we don't provide sales and customer service for other businesses, but we build the tools that allow other businesses to do these things effectively.

A key reason that the company succeeds in providing tools to customer support and sales teams is that it empowers industry professionals to expand the number of contributors who can collaborate in a conversation. Many firms before the rise of Zendesk insisted on the efficiency of assigning one employee resource to one customer contact. Whether selling or supporting, business leaders intuitively viewed customer contacts as an individual effort. If a customer asked you for help, you better find a way to get that customer the help they needed, lest the customer find someone else who could.

But collaborative tools like Zendesk are changing that mindset. Technologies like Zendesk facilitate "intelligence swarming," the integration of the best perspectives into a conversation. Sales and support people can use these technologies to engage multiple collaborators in solving a customer's problems. This mitigates narrow or inaccurate perspectives by increasing the likelihood that the right subject matter experts and the most relevant decision makers are part of the discussion. Support people can consult with an expert before responding to a customer or entirely re-assign the matter to the expert. Salespeople can collaborate with account managers to provide not just pitches but deep insights and genuine solutions. Anyone who builds relationships with customers for a living can take advantage of the collective intelligence of their peers, knowing that they are never alone in their work. Zendesk designed its software with a collaborative philosophy—the idea that a well-connected and collaborative group is more resourceful, effective, and efficient than the steely, siloed resolve of a single mind. The church leader of a tech-shaped culture has an opportunity to embrace collaboration in many ministry areas, but two are particularly important: faith formation and congregational leadership. Today's church leader can align to collaboration as an emerging cultural value by adopting a more collaborative approach to Christian education and by transitioning to a shared leadership model for the congregation's life together.

For reflection and discussion

- Collaborative technology creates opportunities for the inclusion of more perspectives from across the group. Why do you think this might be important in a church?
- What collaborative technologies do you regularly use? Do these technologies create group cohesion and inclusivity? If so, how? If not, why not?
- What might be challenging about using collaborative technology in a ministry context?

Collaboration: ideas for communications	
High-tech	Rather than communicating through a newsletter produced entirely by church staff, build a church "Wiki," or a webpage that all in a community can contribute to. Invite community members to add prayer requests, life announcements, or reflections on where they saw God at work in the world.
Low-tech	Create consistent opportunities for community members to guest-write for newsletters, on blog pages, or on social media. Encourage these guest-writers to describe—through story, image, and video—their involvement in the church's mission.
No-tech	Use dry-erase whiteboards instead of bulletin boards. Rather than posting an announcement to a bulletin board, post it to a whiteboard along with a question for reflection. Invite community members to write or draw a response.

9

Collaboration
and Faith Formation

While I attended seminary, I continued working as an instructional designer in the tech industry. As a training and development professional who has spent considerable time in the classroom outside of my working hours, I am interested in working to resolve the apparent disconnect between how people learn and how churches manage "faith formation," or Christian education. The educational techniques that are part of our tech-shaped culture stand in contrast to many Christian education methods for one reason: while the broader culture has embraced active, collaborative learning, Christian faith formation tends to rely on lectures, sermons, and presentations from experts.

I recognized the extent of that disconnect during a fourth-year course on digital media and ministry. Rather than starting with tactics for using digital media in religious contexts, the course began with some theory on epistemology: what it means to learn and know things. We dove into the philosophy of author and philosopher of education Parker J. Palmer, reading selections from one of his seminal works, *The Courage to Teach*. In the book, Palmer develops the theory that education has long operated within an "objectivist myth" of learning.[1]

This myth falsely teaches us that we learn best from the transmission of inscrutable knowledge, presented through the coherent and organized teachings of a trusted authority. As a consequence, we mistakenly assume that all knowledge is an "object" which we can learn only when we listen to "authorities on high." Submission to this myth heavily influences the way we teach. We teach in a way that demands obedience to authority, respect for order, and submission to hierarchy. It didn't take long for my classmates and me to realize the pervasiveness of this myth in religious settings.

But Palmer challenges this ideology and offers a way forward. He holds that knowing is more subjective than objective, more about the gathering of learners than the gathering of facts. The importance of the subject has profound implications for learning. None can stand atop a hierarchy with an exclusive claim to total understanding of a concept. But we can acknowledge that our points of view are intrinsically incomplete. We can add our vantage points to that of a neighbor, rounding out our shared perspective, and collaborating our way toward greater understanding. According to Palmer, "Knowing of any sort is relational, animated by a desire to come into deeper community with what we know."[2] Learning, whether in the classroom, the workplace, or the church, ought to be a communal and collaborative process.

Palmer's "subjectivist" model is the *modus operandi* of learning in a tech-shaped culture, and especially in the tech industry. This model shows that learning is not about transmission down a hierarchy, but about collaboration and inquiry across a network. My professional contributions as an instructional designer in the tech industry aligns well with Palmer's theory. At Google and at Zendesk, we've sought to create learning environments and training designs that form networks and fosters collaboration among learners. When we review participant survey data (which we fastidiously gather from every single one of our e-Learnings, workshops, or trainings), it's easy to see that our most effective courses are those in which we, the instructors, spend as little time as possible talking at our learners, and as much time as possible allowing learners to experiment, simulate, and practice.

Predictably, learners don't expect or appreciate reading reams of text-based content, just as they don't expect or appreciate lectures. Post-training survey scores have shown us that our least-impactful courses are government-mandated compliance training (the driest example of rote dissemination of content), in which technical facts must be communicated in a standardized method so as to mitigate risk. Conversely, the courses that produce measurable learning outcomes are collaborative workshops in which teams gather around a shared, role-relevant subject (everything from coding to workplace coaching) and work together to build something of their choice (a report, a presentation, and the like) to demonstrate and pass on their learnings.

Our data show that learning is particularly strong when training creates a space for active peer-to-peer teaching. With peer-to-peer teaching, I provide sufficient context about the subject matter (the procedures, the data, the facts, and so forth) and then invite learners to synthesize the subject matter into lessons that they themselves develop. In this way, they can process the subject matter and package it in a way that is applicable to their own context and experience. We've found that learners involved with peer-to-peer teaching don't just glean an awareness of the facts, they build a certain level of confidence in applying the facts to their context.

As Palmer's theory suggests, I find that the more I work in adult learning, the more I find that my job isn't to tell anyone about anything but to build the scaffolding in which individuals can form groups for the purpose of learning from one another. The less text and talking from me, the deeper our learners engage with the course material. As a talent developer, I simply set the subject, provide a minimal amount of background information, and allow the group to do the rest. I've seen this model of learning work for courses on coding, workshops on public speaking, classes on conflict de-escalation, and seminars on email usage. It's worked in large groups and small groups, with senior business leaders and with recent college graduates. Whenever I sit through a one-way training led by an "expert" presenter, I find myself fidgeting, even a little irritated at a lost opportunity for engagement. Wherever I experience training as a collaborative exercise between participants, it leads to deep learning.

Unlike learning in the tech industry, the faith formation I have often observed remains somewhat misaligned with Palmer's theory. According to Palmer, skills are built, confidence is gained, and competencies are acquired through shared action across communities of learners. By extension, his theory might suggest that faith, or trust in God, is never developed passively (though theologians in my Lutheran tradition maintain it is initially acquired through receiving God's Word and the Sacraments). Palmer's model, in which we learn through active collaboration in a network instead of passive consumption within a hierarchy, ought to be the model for faith formation in a tech-shaped culture. I would suggest that faith emerges from grace but then develops through collaborative learning, which leads to faith in action.

Collaborating in the classroom

Christian leaders, faith educators in particular, have an opportunity to align faith formation with the collaborative values of a tech-shaped culture. From the pre-baptismal catechism instructions of the ancient church to the lecture halls of medieval universities and the Sunday school classrooms of today, Christian education has been integral to the

Christian experience. That the high point of many American Protestant worship services is no longer a "sermon" but a "teaching" provides contemporary evidence of the importance of education to the tradition. How, then, might Christian educators create collaborative faith formation experiences?

For starters, the Christian educator must eliminate any use of lecture. The one-way flow of information through lectures is not only misaligned to this cultural moment but has been shown to be ineffective at driving retention.[3] Preachers can preach their sermons in the sanctuary on Sunday, but teachers would do well not to emulate that format. The lecture must especially be dropped from any curriculum meant to engage youth. I know firsthand the brevity of a youth's attention span after a long day of school. I have seen the disinterest when a Christian education class, perhaps a confirmation course or a youth group meeting, demands too much passive listening and not enough active engagement.

Removing the lecture from the curriculum is never as easy as it seems. Ironically, the most lecture-heavy Christian lessons I have ever sat through began with the instructor telling us to "keep it interactive," that "I don't want you to only hear my voice." I typically cringe at such a comment, fully anticipating the deluge of one-way communication that likely comes next. To mitigate this, the Christian educator could carry with them a timer (they likely have one on their phone). They could then measure instructor speaking minutes and contrasting them to learner speaking minutes. If, throughout the class, the instructor lectured at any stretch for more than ten minutes, they would be alerted that they were reducing opportunities for peer to peer learning.

There are many ways to convert Christian education from lecture-listening to collaboration but encouraging learners to teach one another may be the most impactful. Learning theorists have long held that teaching other learners is the instructional design method most directly aligned to retention. In this methodology, the Christian educator pivots from telling everyone what they ought to know, to providing the resources and digitally integrated tools with which learners will develop their own plan for teaching the other learners in the group. Similar to the pastor who curates and creates content for spiritual practice, the Christian educator compiles high-quality resources that students can use to teach one another.

Perhaps instead of lecturing for an hour to a room of eighth graders about the Book of Job (I've seen it done), the instructor shares their expertise by setting the context about the book: the questions it engages, its intended audience, its common contemporary interpretations. They then provide the group with printouts of the key passages in scripture, video resources about the question of suffering in a God-made world, and art supplies for students to build something that reflects what they think of the subject-matter. Instead of an hour of lecture on Job, students spend half the time building on the perspectives of their instructor and others in the class by researching one aspect of the story, its themes, messages, and applications for today. They then create something novel to share with the class that expresses their reaction to and understanding of the material, perhaps a skit, a story, or a game.

When instructors provide the scaffolding and subject matter and create an environment that engages the group in peer-to-peer learning, all are engaged in the collaborative work of Christian education. Our faith formation efforts build active experiences where information will be understood, messages will be reflected on, and faith can be enacted.

Lecture-based and collaborative models of faith formation

Lecture-based model	Collaborative model
Instructor presents all of the subject matter	Instructor provides key information about the subject matter and curated materials for learners to go deeper into the content
Instructor is primary source of instructional content	Curated resources, such as passages from scripture, images, or videos, are primary sources of instructional content
Instructor speaks, learners listen	Instructor supports learners as they explore curated resources
Instructor creates learning objects, such as slides and handouts	Learners create learning objects, such as drawings or writings, based on their reflection.
Instruction concludes with a question-and answer-session, in which the lecturer provides the answers	Instruction concludes with learners sharing what they have created. Other learners are invited to ask questions and share reactions.

Converting lecture-based to collaborative learning experiences

Think of a lecture-based learning experience you have had with Christian education. Reflect on how the experience might have been reshaped to align to a collaborative learning model.

1. What was the subject matter? What core subject matter should the instructor present?
2. What learning question could the instructor have suggested?

3. What resources (passages from scripture, commentaries, videos, photos) could the instructor have curated?
4. What learning objects could the learners have created in response to that question?

Collaboration: ideas for worship	
High-tech	Install a worship "check-in" computer outside the sanctuary or worship center. When attendees arrive on Sunday, they have the option of receiving a randomly assigned worship leadership role. As community members expect to be involved with readings, leading prayers, or offering blessings and benedictions, the cadence of the church's life together becomes more participatory.
Low-tech	Combine prayer and text messaging. During the prayers of the people, invite the congregation to submit petitions to the pastor via SMS. Or, invite the congregation to pray for somebody in their phone contact list. Following the prayer, they text that person to let them know they were prayed for.
No-tech	Use "panel discussion" style preaching. On an occasional Sunday, invite three to four community members to respond to a church leader's questions during a sermon. This is especially useful after a shared event in the life of a community, such as a youth mission trip. The panel questions might focus on where and how they saw God at work.

10

Collaboration and Shared Leadership

Collaborative leadership practices are just starting to break through in Christian communities. Just as it took Google Docs several years to achieve a critical mass of users, so too will it take religious institutions a while to pivot towards more collaborative models of educating and leading.

Sarah Stonesifer Boylan of Virginia Theological Seminary organizes the eFormation Learning Community, a "learning community for ministry in a digital world."[1] A former school librarian, Stonesifer organizes conferences, webinars, and workshops on topics related to faith formation and church leadership in a digital age. According to Stonesifer, church in the digital age requires collaborators far more than it requires communicators; it requires learning facilitators far more than it requires expert lecturers. Faith formation and church leadership alike now require those with a coaching mindset—people, though not necessarily professionalized staff, with skills similar to those found in athletic coaches: setting goals, asking questions, making plans, and adapting where needed. Stonesifer views lay leaders and clergy alike as

Christian coaches, tasked with helping their communities to navigate their spiritual journeys in a hybrid, offline and online, setting. In the digital age, the church leader is a coach, "walking alongside their community in their search for God," she says.[2] Describing the necessary skills of today's church leader, Stonesifer says:

> Today's effective Christian leader is a good collaborator, one who asks the right questions and intentionally listens to help you learn something about yourself. There's no single formula that works for every person or every community. Everyone has a different path, a unique spiritual journey. We need leaders who can ask questions, actively listen, and help us to set an action plan. We need a coach in our search for God to help us find the contours of our own journeys.[3]

In Christian classrooms, learners must become co-teachers. In the Christian movement more broadly, community members must become co-leaders. The hierarchical, pastor as CEO leadership model will not resonate with a tech-shaped culture. Only a collaborative model, where a pastor is one among many called to set a mission and work towards its realization, can align to cultural values.

A collaborative leadership mindset has its roots in core Protestant Reformation doctrine, specifically in Martin Luther's idea of the priesthood of all believers. This doctrine suggests that everyone has access to God through Christ, without mediation by a priest or clergyperson, and that all the faithful are equally called to serve God, the church, their community, and their family. There can be no hierarchy in the church, for all are called to the work of ministry in its myriad forms. The key, then, to replacing more hierarchical forms of leadership with a more collaborative approach is for all the faithful to share in the work of ministry.

Establishing collaborative leadership

Collaboration can take many forms, but it begins with the possibility of an individual offering and receiving feedback and acting together to achieve a common goal. Without a commitment to sharing perspectives and taking action based on shared perspectives, there can be little collaboration at the levels of mission and vision. These fundamental markers of collaboration in a religious community can be framed as questions: To what extent can members of the community share their perspectives with other community members and leaders in a meaningful way? And to what extent can one contribute to the work of the community?

To evaluate the extent of a church's commitment to sharing perspectives and acting together to achieve a common goal, leaders could use a calendar analysis to identify where feedback and involvement are strongest and weakest. To do this, start with a list of the events, activities, and services over the course of a typical week in the ministry. List each of these in the first column of a spreadsheet. Then, form a table by adding the following column headers:

- Was it possible for those involved to share their perspectives?
- Did these perspectives lead to a further conversation, or were any of the perspectives acted on?
- Was collaborative action, or the involvement of many across the community working towards a common goal, possible?
- Was collaborative action taken?

Each of these questions indicates the extent to which the community could and did provide feedback, and the extent to which the community was involved in taking action. Here is an example:

Calendar analysis table

	Was perspective-sharing possible?	Were perspectives actually shared?	Could the sharing of perspectives lead to collaborative action?
Examples: Sunday worship			
Bible study			
Worship planning			
Youth group			

Populate each cell with a yes/no, or with a "1" for yes and a "0" for no. Collaborative ministries will have more "yes" values and a higher "collaborative score."

When feedback and collaborative action are prioritized in a church community, the community is well-positioned to develop a shared leadership model for congregational life. "Shared leadership brings back the priesthood of all believers," says Kristin Wiersma, a ministry consultant focused on helping congregations to improve their leadership practices. Wiersma works with The Joshua Group, a consultancy that partners with churches for the purposes of organizational assessment, strategic planning and visioning, and change management facilitation.[4] For Wiersma, shared leadership starts with community engagement and buy-in. Leaders recognize that "the congregation has a stake in shaping its own future . . . It's a posture of shared vision, shared story, and understanding that the pastor is not the one who determines the mission and vision. It's a posture of appreciation for the many gifts within the community."[5]

Comparing executive-style church leadership with shared leadership

Executive-style leadership	Shared leadership
Mission and purpose determined by select leaders, typically clergy and board	Mission and purpose determined through a collaborative process, with opportunities for widespread involvement
Decisions made by individuals, based on the expertise of persons in leadership and individual consideration of the mission	Decisions made collaboratively, based on the expertise of the group and shared reflection on the mission
Senior leaders are fluent in making business decisions	Senior leaders are fluent in asking coaching questions
Intentional focus on creating an efficient, expert-led organization	Intentional focus on congregational pathways to involvement and succession planning for formalized leadership positions, such as committee chairs, council members, and staff

Churches that adopt shared leadership still have a structure. Ministries need definitions and priorities, and decisions need to be made to keep priorities in focus. To help with the work of adopting a shared leadership model rooted in a shared sense of purpose, Wiersma and her company coach Christians to articulate a clear sense of vision—a shared answer to the question of "why" the church exists. Everyone in the community is invited to help discern its shared vision. Surveys are sent, focus groups are held, conversations are started.

My home congregation has recently begun to adopt a shared leadership model. Within this model, we've tasked the congregation with generating aspirations for the direction of the ministry and the board with discerning a mission and vision from those aspirations.

To the pastors, we have given the traditional Lutheran markers of ordination: proclamation of the Word and the administration of the Sacraments. At the heart of this model is the simple message that all who are gathered matter, that all gifts are invaluable to God's mission, and that all involvement is meaningful to the vitality of the ministry.

When the model is fully in place, anyone interested in the community can walk through the doors and easily get involved. Simple mechanisms are in place to take these ideas and convert them into actions carried out by volunteer teams within the congregation. Listening sessions are scheduled for board members and staff to intentionally listen to perspectives of church members and leaders in the broader community who are not affiliated with the congregation. Church staff continuously solicit feedback and input from the congregation—on worship, service, communications, and other aspects of community life—and develop and reshape their ministry based on it. Board meeting minutes and write-ups of decisions affecting the congregation are transparently shared and communicated. Community members are coached to discern their role in the shared mission, to contribute their unique gifts to what God is calling the church to be.

Reflecting on the vision and mission of the organization, a leader should then engage the community in determining first steps toward greater collaboration. This could be as rudimentary as installing a "suggestion box" outside the sanctuary or worship center. It might be as digitally sophisticated as distributing a satisfaction survey to the congregation via a church newsletter or congregation app. It could be as audacious as committing to greater shared leadership during worship: having prayers led by a community member or even lay preaching! Start with a small first step toward greater collaboration because success with these first steps will lead to collaboration on the bigger projects of mission, vision, and purpose.

The best indicator of successful collaboration in the church is the extent to which the community can work together to set, revise, and commit to its mission. For this reason, it is critical for church leaders to regularly engage the community in conversations about its central identity and call from God. As our digital technologies predispose culture toward collaboration, collaboration must become the operating principle of church, not at a superficial level, but at the foundational levels of mission and purpose.

A mission is simply a statement, drafted by the community, that specifies its purpose for being. A mission statement is tactical yet aspirational, grounded yet lofty. It pulls together the ideals of shared action with the particulars of life together. So many in my generation are open to the idea of church but can't answer, *why making the trip to a sanctuary on a Sunday is worth our time.* Kristin Wiersma observes, "People don't fall in love with a building or bureaucracy anymore, and they won't commit to perpetuating the existence of an organization. They fall in love with mission. They fall in love with purpose."[6] A widely known, collaboratively determined sense of mission is the key to a vibrant church in a digital, unchurched age.

Wiersma identifies many reasons the collaborative development of mission is central to the church of the digital age, but one I feel particularly drawn to is that the process fosters spiritual development. "Setting a mission lets people ask what God has called us here to do," she says. "To set a mission, you must start by telling faith stories and call stories . . . It's important that people develop that language of faith on their lips, and have names for God, and can talk about what God is up to in their lives . . . The more they talk about [it], the more they are aware of God's work in their vocations and in their community."[7]

A strong and shared sense of mission answers the question *why* God called this community to exist. In a culture where membership is no longer normative, no religious organization can exist without answering this question. The challenge for church leaders in a tech-shaped culture is not merely to develop a mission statement, but to develop a statement collaboratively after a congregation's leaders (both lay and ordained, staff and non-staff) complete an intensive period of listening and discernment that includes the congregation's members and neighbors. For example, a congregation in my hometown recently engaged school administrators in their mission-setting process in an attempt to connect the work of the church with the well-being of neighborhood students.

Once a statement is drafted, it must be clearly and consistently communicated. In this digital age, communities turn over quickly and change in the population is constant. It's essential that all who enter into a community, for however brief a time, are aware of that community's purpose. People can contribute to that purpose only when they know what it is. Accordingly, the congregation's mission statement should be widely known, it should be at the center of the community's life together. I once visited a congregation that incorporated their mission statement into the benediction at the conclusion of every Sunday service. It was also printed in their worship bulletin, atop their website, and on a banner hung over the door to the sanctuary. The congregation was and is a small worshipping community by its denominational standards, but its sense of purpose and the people's collaboration towards that purpose was strong and significant.

Of course, it's important to constantly and collectively ideate, write, rewrite, and solicit feedback based on those ideas. Any congregation needs a collaborative process for defining, living out, and redefining its mission. A congregation's sense of mission should be revisited in times of conflict (as a means of centering the community in what really matters), in times of strategic planning, in times of great change, or in seasons of low engagement. As each of these situations tends to draw Christian communities inward, they present opportunities to reflect on how God is still calling the church outward. The test of a mission is not its longevity, but the extent to which it inspires a congregation or community to intentionally listen for and actively respond to God's call. As Wiersma suggests, "Strategic renewal, done together, is the only insurance against irrelevance."[8]

Quiz: Is your congregation's mission statement collaborative?

1. Our congregation/community regularly communicates and reminds people about our mission statement. Yes ○ No ○

2. The majority of the members in our congregation/community have memorized the mission statement or can paraphrase it if requested. Yes ○ No ○

3. The group responsible for drafting the mission statement included clergy, staff, lay leaders, congregation members, and community members. Yes ○ No ○

4. The group responsible for drafting the mission statement held listening sessions with clergy, staff, lay leaders, congregation members, and community members. Yes ○ No ○

5. The group responsible for drafting the mission statement tested several plausible alternatives. Yes ○ No ○

6. When strategic renewal is deemed necessary, the congregation has a process for revising the statement. Yes ○ No ○

For reflection and discussion

- To what extent was our mission statement developed through a collaborative process?
- What could be done to more consistently communicate the mission statement?
- When might we need to consider revising the statement?

Deepening collaboration by design

Given the ever-changing nature of mission, church leaders should be fluent in the process of design thinking. At its core, design thinking is a method a group uses to creatively and systemically solve a problem.[9] It is widely used in the technology industry, but it need not be confined to the worlds of tech or business. It can be used for software development, process creation, or even for weight loss and personal organization! Design thinking engages all four cultural values of the digital age. It begins with a big research question (in the church, "what is our calling or purpose?" is a suitable question) and ideates and tests possible answers. It is constantly collaborative, and like all creative efforts, requires considerable idea generation and even more idea refinement. Design thinking is a concrete and widely used habit that churches ought to use in collaboratively responding to and articulating God's call—in setting, living, and resetting their mission. Focused on the gifts and opportunities within a faith community, design thinking offers a structured, pragmatic process for turning a church community outward for service to the neighbor.

While other methods exist, the promise of design thinking comes from its scalability—its effectiveness for both organizations and individuals—and its impact across all varieties of industries. Design thinking is an effective problem-solving technique for a tech-shaped culture because it provides a process for a group to be creative and innovative while remaining grounded in the particulars of its context.

Design thinking offers a compelling antidote to hierarchical decision making and groupthink.

It all starts with a powerful question capable of generating conversation, action, and solutions. In the world of tech, the question could be, "What is the most effective website design for users who need help with our product?" In the world of church, it ought to be a question such as, "What mission has God called us to?" or "How is God calling us together to serve the needs of this community?" While this step seems simple and intuitive, it's essential not to rush through the question formation. Every subsequent step in design thinking comes back to this original research question.

Once the research question is defined, the next step of the design thinking process is to define stakeholder or customer "requirements." In the mission-setting process, requirements encompass the passions, interests, and needs within a Christian community. In the tech world, defining requirements involves talking to users, connecting with engineers, and understanding market opportunities. But in the church world, defining requirements involves walking the neighborhood, listening deeply to community members' stories, empathizing with them, and resisting the inclination to offer simplistic answers. Gathering requirements is not about identifying solutions, it's about defining opportunities and gifts. It's about empathizing, not advocating—listening, not speaking. As a collaborative endeavor, the needs of and gifts within a community are never determined by clergy alone. They need to be determined by the shared leadership of the church, pastors, parishioners, and community leaders alike, working together as co-equal research anthropologists. Again, the tendency of the second step in design thinking is to rush through and document what is already known. The effective church community takes their time in the research process, committing themselves to deep and active listening. In many cases, the actual needs within a community have root causes that are both complex, nuanced, and quite different from initial assumptions.

Developing a mission statement

Phase of Design Thinking Process	Practices for Mission Development
Determine the research question	Collaboratively consider the question: "What is God calling us here to do?"
Determine requirements	Listen and empathize. What are the opportunities in this congregation and the surrounding neighborhood that God is calling us to address? What are gifts, talents, and resources that the community can harness to address those opportunities?
Document and share	Communicate findings with the congregation
Collaboratively brainstorm	Reflect and write several possible statements
Test	Consider whether the statements align to the gifts and opportunities within the congregation. Consider whether such a purpose would inspire action given the opportunities in the community. Solicit feedback!
Share the mission statement	Communicate the final mission statement so it is deeply known by all in the congregation and is known within the surrounding neighborhood

After the needs of the community are researched, identified, documented by church leaders, and shared throughout the congregation, the design thinking process proceeds to a collaborative brainstorm. In the tech world, this is when the team comes up with new products and processes for meeting user needs. In the church, this is when the community prays, reflects, and begins to write. In this phase, the group will determine multiple viable ideas, or in the context of church, many possible variations of an eventual mission statement. Those possibilities are written down before the group temporarily adjourns for reflection and rejuvenation.

The fourth phase of design thinking is testing. In tech, the testing phase involves building prototypes of software or a process, holding up the prototypes to the initial requirements, and measuring alignment. At church, testing involves reflecting on whether such a mission matches the congregation's gifts and talents and aligns with identified ministry opportunities. How would the church operate, given its mission? Who would it serve? How would it structure its life together? A key deliverable of testing is a sense of feasibility, so here, then, is another important question: Given the resources available, especially people's time and energy, to what extent is the proposed statement compelling enough to inspire action and energy while also feasible enough to be put into practice?

The final steps of the design thinking process are sharing and storytelling—choosing one prototype (version of the mission statement) after an extensive period of feedback, and making that statement widely known. Rarely is one of the initial prototypes chosen in its entirety. The decision is never made by a single decision-maker. All interested parties in the church—and ideally, the wider community—are to be given an opportunity to respond to the proposed prototypes. Through listening sessions and surveys, the prototypes are evaluated through surveys and discussion questions and reshaped until the community emerges with a clearly defined sense of call. The final product of mission development by way of design thinking is the statement itself, the sentence articulating all that the church will be for the foreseeable future. It is a clear statement of Christ's action in the community and the community's commitment to a shared and collaborative response.

A collaborative frontier

The church of a tech-shaped culture will be a collaborative church, a learning community of servant leaders with a strong sense of mission. This future will not come about easily. A commitment to collaboration is a commitment to changing our faith formation practices as we make our learning more participatory. A commitment to collaboration is a commitment to shared leadership as clergy and staff leaders pivot from the role of executive to the role of coach. Collaboration requires audacious change-managers who are bold enough to trust God's action in the community, wise enough to balance their own expertise with community input, and reflective enough to remain grounded in the community's holy purpose. When pursued with intentionality and commitment, collaboration will turn a church outward in response to God's call to love and serve the neighbor.

For reflection and discussion

- To what extent does this church facilitate feedback and shared action?
- How confident and clear is this church in its sense of mission?
- How deeply is collaboration valued within this church? Where and when has this community collaborated meaningfully with groups outside of the church?
- What three specific actions would strengthen this community's sense of shared leadership?

Collaboration: ideas for communications	
High-tech	Create a "perspectives sharing" section on a church app or mobile website. Use push notifications to encourage community members to provide feedback on experiences or share stories in response to a community discussion.
Low-tech	Use video to tell stories of the church's mission statement in action, helping the congregation understand what the mission looks like at a concrete level. Show the videos before or after worship services and share on social media.
No-tech	Use the design thinking process to set and revise the church's mission statement.

SECTION 4
CREATIVITY

. . . .

Thanks to YouTube, it's never been easier to record, broadcast, and share our stories. A one-time competitor to the now defunct Google Video, YouTube was acquired into the Google family of products in 2006 at a price tag of $1.65 billion.[1] Its initial acquisition price now seems a bargain. YouTube generates upwards of four billion dollars in revenue per year.[2] There's a reason for its success: YouTube is, without a doubt, the world's greatest storytelling engine.

From a content creator's perspective, a post to YouTube is a prime-time broadcast to the worldwide web. The shareable and embeddable nature of the platform extends its reach far beyond YouTube itself. Once you upload your story, you can Tweet it to your followers, email it to your colleagues, embed it within a presentation, or stream it on your television screen. The democratic core of YouTube is what inspires content creators around the world to upload an average of 400 hours of video every single minute of every single day.[3] Videos that attract a certain threshold of viewers can even generate revenue for their creators, further incentivizing the content creation process.

To viewers, YouTube offers news stories, sports highlights, educational content, user-generated commentary, and myriad other types of video content accessible via online search. Accordingly, YouTube is now the world's second-largest search engine (behind only Google. com).[4] Each day, over 1.9 billion YouTube viewers access the platform to watch, listen, and laugh, engaging with over 1 billion hours of video content.[5] Viewers also go to YouTube to learn. The platform's top-four most viewed categories are "comedy, music, entertainment/pop culture, and 'how to.'"[6] If it weren't for YouTube, I would still have a dripping kitchen faucet, a bicycle with a wobbly back wheel, a front lawn infested with ants, and a gas grill that catches fire anytime I am cooking brat-wurst. YouTube stories have influenced my personal life, my professional development, and my spirituality. It's continually expanded my perspectives, bringing stories and voices into my life that never would have made it through the rigors of broadcast cable. As a storytelling engine, YouTube is democratizing the creative process. A tech-shaped culture expects opportunities to be creative, to build and share experiences, often in the form of a story. The church of a tech-shaped culture will be a workshop for creativity, a forum for the sharing of stories.

11

Encountering Christ through Creating

The digital age empowers artists to share their work with a larger audience and assess their reaction. This sharing is facilitated by tools like Blogger, Pinterest, and Instagram, which invite viewers into a broader conversation about the work than what was previously possible. These platforms broaden the reach of artistic expression, extending the artist's ability to express the inexpressible. The arts offer a powerful alternative to the dogma and doctrine that my unchurched generation was raised with. The church of the digital age will help communities to encounter Christ not through words alone but through opportunities for creative expression.

I first came to this realization as I was nodding off in a post-lunch stupor one dark January afternoon at Luther Seminary. A youth ministry professor remarked that the future of the church would be shaped not just by the preachers or the theologians but by the artists. He argued that musicians, poets, painters, and writers would ignite experiences of God and facilitate encounters with the divine. The logic and rhetoric of the preacher would have a place in the digital-age church, but the creative process would be foundational to the search for God. Artists' work, and their new capacity to share their work, would help to reanimate the gospel message for a generation uninterested in words, reason, and doctrine. I nodded along, then returned to translating the Greek verbs in Paul's letter to the Philippians. This, after all, was a necessary task if my term paper was to be based on a logical and coherent biblical argument.

The professor's comment stuck with me, in part because, like the gospel message, the arts have mattered a great deal to me, but I have never counted myself as an artist. I always saw art as a professional, technical skill—a special aptitude for activities like painting and sculpting. Those who were artistic were born to be artistic, and we know they were born to be artistic because their visual artwork shows us as much. The artists were the students who attended special camps over summer vacation, the kids whose paintings hung framed in the high school hallway. As a football player with an aptitude for music and language, but certainly not for portraits or landscapes, I knew that I was not part of that clique. The demarcation between "artists" and "non-artists" remains with me. I still struggle to separate the artistic process from the visual arts or to view as artists anyone without a demonstrated skill in disciplines like drawing and painting. I still view my own skills as a musician and a writer as "hobby" interests—but not actual artistic skill.

Maybe some of this has to do with the way art is taught in the American school system. Art is a specific academic subject quite different from music and literature—taught by a different teacher, at a different time of the day, in a different classroom. The students who excel under the tutelage of that specific teacher, at that given time and location, are said to be good at art. One who makes a remarkable clay pot as a kindergartner is said to be an emerging talent. One whose clay pot explodes in the kiln due to a failure to follow directions is said to have other gifts. In high school, when art courses are no longer mandatory in many school districts, the artistic process becomes even more specialized, ossifying the divide between artists and non-artists. The art students become even more of a clique. They paint, they sculpt, they design the sets for the musicals. Non-artists like me sit behind or beneath the sets, playing an instrument backstage as a part of the pit orchestra in *Jesus Christ Superstar*.

All of us *are* artists

On the blustery January afternoon of my twenty-first birthday, my head pounding from the night before, I boarded an Alitalia flight and took off to spend a semester in Tuscany. January, the month of my arrival, is not a beautiful month in Tuscany. It rains almost every day. The temperatures are cool—not cold, like in my native Wisconsin, but damp and generally unpleasant. As a result, few tourists venture to see the wonders of Florence—the Uffizi, the Galleria, the *palazzi* (palaces), or the *piazzi* (public squares).

During these winter months, students have the museums entirely to themselves. With few tourists in sight, I had unfettered access to truly magnificent art: some as visible as the Duomo itself, other works hidden, like Fra Angelico's icons traced on the walls of monastic cloisters. Though I didn't know it at the time, the hours I spent strolling the cavernous galleries of Florence would turn out to be among the most spiritually meaningful moments of my life. I was transfixed by the light on the water in Da Vinci's *Baptism of Christ*, the golden mosaics on the roof of the Florence Baptistery, the penitential gaze of Ghiberti's *John the Baptist*. But the effect the art had on me transcended mere aesthetics.

There's a complex political and economic history behind the Florentine artistic heritage, much of it involving the Medici family's desire to be forgiven of the medieval sin of usury and their desire to finance art as penance. Still, subtle spiritual questions saturate the art. Questions about the fully divine, fully human nature of Christ. Questions about the importance of Mary to the Christian story. Questions about judgment and salvation (a bit of an obsession among early Renaissance mosaicists!), about pathos and redemption, about why Christ had to die and what the resurrection means for us. In Florence, the conflicted faces of the disciples, the expressions of the crucified Messiah, and the subtle aspirations of the virgin mother taught me that the search for God inevitably transcends language.

I now understand that in order to grow in faith, it is sometimes necessary to ask questions in a conversation that goes beyond the words. Donatello, Michelangelo, and Raphael are masters not because of their aptitude in the visual arts but because their masterpieces ignited a dialogue that stretches into today. To see their works in person is not to march towards certainty but to be invited to contemplate the inexpressible truths of God's work in our world. That's why creativity can be a spiritual practice, and why church leaders need to create space for artistic expression.

I subscribe to Father Richard Rohr's daily newsletter. His words provide so many people with a refreshing perspective on the Christian faith in a time of great change. In 2018, Rohr dedicated a week of newsletter entries to art and the creative process. Among my favorite lines from that series: "Our divine DNA carries the creative impulse of the Creator. Even if you don't consider yourself creative or artistic, it is an inherent part of your being."[1] Father Rohr goes on to describe the capacity of art to transcend dualism, to challenge our assumptions and certainty, and to "amplify the sacred." Viewing art is an act of spiritual searching. Creating art is an act that propels us forward in our search. In the digital age, we aren't just viewers. We are all artists.

We are all artists because that is exactly what God created us to be. The first chapter of Genesis describes God not as a monarch, an almighty ruler, or an all-knowing judge, but as a creator (Genesis 1:1), who "created mankind in God's own image" (Genesis 1:27). Part of the *imago dei* that all of us share is God's inclination to create. From the beginning, Genesis attests to the original goodness in God's creation. From the beginning, God made us to go forth and do likewise.

Some movements in the history of Christianity have grasped this idea more easily than others. The Protestant tradition has at best an ambivalent relationship with the arts. The Reformation as a historical event is hardly known for its contributions to artistic endeavor. It's usually remembered for the opposite. Followers of the iconoclast movement that grew out of the Reformation destroyed religious art, hurling priceless works into bonfires with accusations that the works were expressions of idolatry and other sinfulness. Andreas Karlstadt and John Calvin were among the most influential theologians of the time. They were also its most notorious destroyers of statues and images.

Martin Luther, the father of the Reformation movement, couldn't fathom this destructive impulse. He was the anti-iconoclast. While he refused to classify the commissioning of art as a "good work" meriting salvation, he saw with great clarity how artistic creation deepens our engagement with the scriptures. As his contemporaries were stripping altars and toppling statues, he remarked:

> It is possible for me to hear and bear in mind the story of the Passion of our Lord. But it is impossible for me to hear and bear it in mind without forming mental images of it in my heart. For whether I will or not when I hear of Christ, an image of a man hanging on a cross takes form in my heart just as a reflection of my face naturally appears in the water when I look into it.[2]

Luther understood faith to have a visual and creative component. While he held that art didn't create faith, he believed art is important to faith formation. For Luther, art is a "pedagogical" element of our search for God. That's part of the reason the early Lutheran tradition embraced religious art, even when their Protestant counterparts were busy burning "idols."

I learned in Italy that art does not belong to a gifted class of skilled individuals. In the age of Blogger and Instagram, we are artists because creativity connects us to God and to one another in ways that no Bible study or sermon ever will. Looking for clarity in your search for God? Stop thinking and start creating. Continue questioning but direct your questions through a creative medium. Paint your questions. Sculpt them. Build them with pipe cleaners into a diorama. Then, share what you have created. Find a trusted audience and let your work speak to them. By creating, sharing, and listening for reaction, you join the spirit-driven tradition of da Vinci and Rembrandt, of Vasari and Botticelli. It matters not whether you're any good. It matters not whether you see yourself as a true artist. It just matters that you create.

Given that we are all artists, then, what would happen if churches became artistic workshops, gathering places not only for listening to weekly sermons but for the creative expression of our journeys in all of their uniqueness? What if we liberated crayons and paints from the closets of the Sunday school and turned them over to the entire congregation, even to the broader community? How much richer would our churches be?

"Church as workshop" wouldn't even be all that difficult to implement. Try it in your church's confirmation program or youth group. Read a short passage of scripture. Take a moment for contemplative prayer. Then turn the listeners lose to respond through art. Play some music—not just hymns or stale "Christian rock" recordings—but spiritually thought-provoking works that complement the artistic process. This experiment may involve a turn away from the Newsboys and Mercy Me, and a turn toward the perspective-expanding meditations of George Harrison or the soul-searching ballads of U2. It may involve encouraging creators to share their works with the world. But if everyone in a congregation is given a regular chance to do the same, they will learn to speak of faith in a language that transcends words.

"I describe some of what our church does as a community art project," says Pastor Keith Anderson. "When we're planning to do something, I think about how we might create and produce something together. It doesn't matter if what we create together is excellent. What matters is that we create and participate."

The challenge of Christian art

While art and creativity have become important spiritual disciplines, art and contemporary Christianity are sometimes at odds. When I was in high school, I used to attend a large, four-day Christian rock festival. I looked forward to it every summer. I love live music and have always appreciated a lively, outdoor concert atmosphere. But when I look back on this festival, it all feels a bit inauthentic. Every night, some casually dressed speaker would come out and speak. Sometimes they'd get kids to laugh, often they'd get kids to cry. Sometimes they'd get us all to feel rather bad about ourselves. Actor Kirk Cameron was likely the speaker most adept at spraying shame from the stage. His speech emphasized the total and utter depravity of humanity, casting a demoralizing pall over the concert-goers. I found his remarks a bit heavy, but I was a fan of his work from *Growing Pains*. I still have a frisbee with Kirk Cameron's signature on it tucked away in my basement.

After these speeches, a Christian rock band would show up. Usually, the band was one of international acclaim, one whose songs were regularly on the Christian rock station and whose albums were available at all Christian bookstores. They'd play a few tunes, get us to raise our hands toward the sky, say a few prayers over us. All this was done with the utmost attention to production quality. The sound, the lights, the special effects were carefully coordinated to amplify the music and glorify Jesus. Despite the sold-out venues and the packed seating near the main stage, I can't help but feeling that this entire show was spiritually hollow—that it was far more of a sales pitch for a Jesus "brand" than a creative expression of an inexpressible encounter with the divine. It all felt a bit contrived, more like a four-day infomercial for the church and its affiliate industries than an expression of Christian creativity.

Creativity matters to our spiritual identity. But genuine creativity requires us to build something that is authentic to our search for God, not to consume something that has been mass-produced. As Michael Gungor of The Liturgists Podcast wrote in a 2013 article for Relevant Magazine:

> If art's primary purpose is to sell something, it moves away from art and becomes primarily a marketing tool. Similarly, if art's primary purpose is to convince someone of an idea by manipulating his or her emotions, then that art becomes mere propaganda . . . Good Christian art is simply good art—art that explores and expresses our deepest and truest humanity, art that speaks to us, prods us, inspire us.[3]

A tech-shaped culture assumes and enables authentic creativity. When we create something artistic, we participate in God's ongoing work of creating what is good and original. We immerse ourselves in a process that has been central to the Christian story, from the beginning and into today. We engage the image of God within us, a creative impulse that will define what it means to be church throughout the digital age.

For reflection and discussion

- What types of art are most visible in our Christian community (music, painting, sculpture, others)?
- What does this say about who creates art?

- What does this art say about our understanding of art and its place in the church?
- What would it look like for our church to encourage an entire community to participate in the creative process?

Creativity: ideas for church leadership	
High-tech	Create a YouTube series that explores stories of the community's mission statement in action. Frequently promote the series as a means of helping the congregation to understand how they can meaningfully contribute.
Low-tech	Use mind-mapping software like Coggle or LucidChart to guide brainstorming sessions in council and committee meetings. Mind-mapping encourages leaders to make connections that may have previously been difficult to access.
No-tech	Develop empathy and understanding with the neighborhood. Begin leadership meetings by providing a space for those in the neighborhood surrounding the church to share their own stories, not just related to faith, but related to the everyday needs and dreams of individuals from the community.

12

Creating Faith through Story

While "art" encompasses many different disciplines, one particular artform is already familiar to Christian communities of the digital age: the art of storytelling. In my work as a training and development professional and my experiences in ministry, I've come to recognize the extent to which people in our tech-shaped culture learn through telling and listening to stories. As an instructional designer, I've seen an entire cottage industry emerge to help corporate trainers like me to incorporate more storytelling into our instructional designs. Workplace trainers can get certifications in storytelling, attend webinars on stories in e-Learning, and travel to conferences to hear about the use of narrative in compliance courses. They can subscribe to podcasts about storytelling in business contexts and enroll in graduate-level seminars on teaching through narrative. They can take classes on storytelling with PowerPoint or download infographics on how to convert time-intensive courses into succinct and snappy digital stories. Ten percent of all breakout sessions at the 2019 Association for Talent Development's International Conference and Exposition, the training industry's largest annual conference, were dedicated exclusively to story. Dozens of books, and likely thousands of blog posts, sell the intuitive idea that we learn not by focusing on facts but by immersing our minds in narrative.

Storytelling is a form of creativity that benefits the teller as much as the listener. By translating abstraction into everyday language that is grounded in experience, we learn from the creative process of telling our own stories. One of my preferred methods for training is to invite participants to listen to a podcast interview, a recorded conversation snippet with someone who is doing something innovative. Maybe the interviewee has written a basic script to automate a mundane task. Perhaps they've figured out an effective way to give feedback in the right moments or found an extracurricular opportunity to learn a new professional skill. Whatever their story of innovation, I ask them about it and share that story with the company. Using a low-cost USB microphone and a laptop, I interview coworkers for five minutes, distributing these audio stories via email newsletter.

If my co-workers are uncertain how to share their experience, I offer them an easy, three-step framework that appears in many good stories, whether they are about using technology or defeating evil empires in outer space: situations, complication, and resolution. And so I ask them: How were you going about your day-to-day work? What did you decide needed fixing and why? What did you do to improve the situation, and how does that help you today? Basic questions lead to easy answers that provide gripping, or at least compelling, narratives. It's not just the listeners who have something to learn from this experience. Those who take the time to articulate their stories solidify their own learning, further reinforcing their confidence with the subject matter.

Churches as storytelling workshops

Just as learning in a tech-shaped culture requires the opportunity to reflect, construct, and share a story, in addition to the opportunity to hear the stories of others, faith formation in the digital age has a similar set of requirements. We live, learn, and encounter Christ through stories. And with digital platforms providing new opportunities to create and share those experiences, the church of the digital age will align Christianity's long-revered stories with new stories unique to the community. Churches should start to align to a tech-shaped culture by thinking critically about the stories they tell, and who creates them, shares them, and hears them.

It seems to me that leaders in many congregations, particularly worship planners and educators, have responded to recent declines in church attendance by focusing on polishing the performance of a limited number of stories. We've swapped out the organ and brought in the electric guitar and drum set, moved out the hymnals and installed high-tech projectors and screens. We've dropped the clerical garb and replaced it with stylish sneakers and skinny jeans. We've installed better sound systems, experimented with lighting, and even removed the pulpit so the preacher can be at the same level as the people. All of these changes have improved the performative aspects of a story that is usually told by a select few. But we should have instead been focused on helping those in the community to reflect, articulate, and share their experiences. We should have been focused on building Christian communities known not for excellent performance, but for widespread creativity. We should have been providing workshops for those in the community to tell their own stories.

Why workshops? Because everyone who walks into a church has a story to tell. Everyone with a smartphone and a YouTube app has an easy way to share it. Some people even assume, explicitly or not, that their story is worth sharing. A few are even audacious enough to want to tell it. By asking someone to share their story of faith, church leaders give that individual the space to contemplate how God is working through their lives—and affirm that God is indeed at work! Today's

135

church leaders should think of their work less as CEOs and more as Chief Storytelling Officers. The job description is simple and has two main duties: Build your parishioners' confidence in their ability to tell their own story so as to increase their willingness to do so. Then give them the opportunity to tell it.

Their story doesn't have to be particularly persuasive, nor does it need to be recorded digitally and set to mellow background music. It doesn't have to be a conversion story. It probably shouldn't be an airing of the proverbial dirty laundry, though there may be a time and place for sharing such experiences. It just needs to be human. The story can be as simple as a reflection on where we see God at work in our professional lives, in our family ties, even in our church! Stories can be creative responses to something that is tangible or even mundane.

I helped to produce a congregational podcast recently built around congregation members describing a song that was meaningful to their walk with Christ. Members wrote and recorded stories about music, from Bach to U2. It was our experience that the community was eager to share their stories and grateful for the opportunity to creatively express their faith.

Many church leaders are starting to recognize the relationship between spirituality and creativity, exploring what it means to grow in faith by telling our stories. Dave Daubert is a pastor and consultant who believes that stories can form our faith and shape our experience of God, provided we have opportunities to create them and share them. He says:

> To form a faith community around stories, start by asking very simple questions that lead to the articulation of experience. Ask questions like, what's your favorite hymn and why do you like it? The hymn they choose isn't nearly as important as why they chose it—that's where the story is. Or ask questions like, who brought you to have you baptized, and why

did they do it? These simple questions get people to articulate their spiritual journey. They help people to tell their story.

Daubert sees the role of the pastor as one who facilitates the telling of stories. "Church leaders need to consistently ask faith-focused questions that everyone has an opportunity to answer," says Daubert. "If you want [people] to tell stories, you have to ask good questions. Because the answer to every good question can always be a good story."[1]

Pastor Keith Anderson, co-author of *Click2Save*, also appreciates the contributions that storytelling makes to faith formation. "The advice I would give to any church is to use technology to tell and retell stories," he says.[2] "Church is about relationships—and relationships are forged through stories. Digital media provides a great platform for telling creative, compelling stories—and listening to the stories of others."

Anderson and his congregation, Upper Dublin Lutheran in Ambler, Pennsylvania, develop, produce, and distribute digital stories about faith journeys. He explains:

> We use technology to give people a platform. One of our recent projects was a podcast based on the book *We Make the Road by Walking*. In each episode, I recorded a 15-minute interview with a member of the congregation talking about a chapter of the book and what it means in their lives. It was like a congregational book study—but in podcast form. I was the host, and as host, my job was to elevate the stories in our congregation.

Pastor Keith is quick to point out that the work of digital storytelling is not technically complex. "Anyone can record a conversation. Anyone can produce a podcast. Our role as church leaders is to set the stage for you to come in and share your ideas."

The church of a tech-shaped culture will be a storytelling church, where church leaders provide opportunities for the community to share their experiences. Church leaders will provide space for all to tell stories about the places they visited where God felt close, about specific moments in their lives where God felt near, or moments in their lives when God felt distant. Through videos, podcasts, and art projects, these stories will be a central, visible marker of a community's life together.

The promise of lay preaching

One place where these stories need to become increasingly visible is the pulpit. In many faith traditions, we've been letting pastors speak nearly every Sunday for hundreds of years, muting the stories of the community in favor of the stories from the clergy. It's time to explore what it would look like to make the pulpit another visible indicator of a community's commitment to creativity through story.

"Make sure the pastor's not the only one speaking, and when the pastor is preaching, try to make some space for non-scripted dialogue," says Daubert. "That's where people learn. Those sermons are the most memorable. As church leaders, we need to stop coming out of the seminary and telling people about the Gospel. We need to start equipping, helping, and coaching people to articulate the experience of the Gospel in their lives. Sometimes, the most compelling stories are interviews with a parishioner. Sometimes, it's more traditional lay preaching. But the era when one pastor preached fifty-two sermons a year is over."

It's impossible to be a storytelling church if the sermon, the primary storytelling mechanism in institutional Christianity, continues to be monopolized by the clergy. Lay preaching is Christian storytelling at its most authentic. To open a congregation to lay preaching is to affirm that the stories of the laity and clergy alike matter, to show the breadth and depth of God's work through each of us.

Preaching a sermon as a lay person is a profoundly impactful experience. As a lay minister, I have found nothing so spiritually formative as the process of reflecting on a text, seeing where it intersects with my own life story, and shaping a narrative in response. Though preaching can be time-consuming and mentally fatiguing, the act of writing and preaching a sermon provides space for us to reflect and concretely demonstrate where God is active in our lives.

"I think preaching is so important to our spirituality," says Darleen Pryds, associate professor of Christian spirituality and history at the Franciscan School of Theology.[3] Dr. Pryds studies and teaches Franciscan history and has written extensively about the rich tradition of Franciscan lay preaching.

Pryds is a lay preacher herself. "Nothing immerses me in a biblical text like preaching. I don't go to that level of engagement unless I'm wrestling with a passage while writing a sermon. We learn so much by creating. Even though it can be difficult, and sometimes uncomfortable, our spiritual lives need the deep, thoughtful reflection that comes with preparing and preaching a sermon."

Among the courses she teaches in Southern California is Lay Spiritual Practices, a class on the history of "spiritual activities used by lay Christians." The course immerses students in a range of practices including "pilgrimage, prayer, contemplation, storytelling, fasting, feasting, sexuality and celibacy, festivals and processions."[4] A focus of the course is lay preaching.

"For most of my students, which range in age from twenty-two to seventy-five, it's the first time they preach. Whatever their age, they all take a great amount of satisfaction from the opportunity. They go to the chapel with the rest of their class, and they can preach how they want to," says Pryds. "The most memorable preaching is based on their own lives. It's never exegetical. Telling their stories is very transformational—for both the preacher, and the listener."

Telling a shared story

Preaching is not the only way for individuals to exercise their creativity. Jim Keat is the Minister of Design and Digital Strategy at The Riverside Church in New York. A self-described "ideation specialist" and an "aspiring minimalist," Pastor Keat seeks to lift up the faith stories of those with whom he ministers. Keat begins his ministry with the conviction that faith in the digital age is formed by broadcasting one's narrative. "Churches so often see the internet as a broadcast tool. We [think we] just have to post events—as if the media just exists for sharing links," says Keat.[5] "But the point of new media is not to get someone to walk into your building."

Keat suggests that the best usage of digital media is as a platform for "creating and sharing." Keat, a prolific creator of digital content, has used YouTube for interviews with parishioners and for sermon streaming. He's used YouTube for children's messages and for meditations. He's been a podcaster, filmmaker, and social media professional—all with the intent of telling the Gospel story. One of his most interesting YouTube-based projects is titled *Thirty Seconds or Less*. It's a collection of short stories, each lasting half a minute or less, each submitted by a different "storyteller." Members of his congregations and major figures in contemporary Christianity have contributed their stories to this collection of short videos. Topics range from activism to mindfulness to the Enneagram. Some stories are retellings of a book of the Bible. In one of Keat's videos, prolific Christian storyteller Rob Bell describes Leviticus, summarizing the book of laws with the hopeful message "Your life matters."

"Digital age ministry is just curation done well," says Jim. "Ministry in a digital age is about finding stories and ideas and putting them together. Everyone is a creator. The church should be the curator. It's about remixing, repackaging, and sharing the stories of your community."

In the summer of 2019, Pastor Jim Keat packed all of his possessions into an Airstream trailer and took to the highways for an extended road trip. He'll still serve as the Minister of Design and Digital Strategy at The Riverside Church, but his calling has gone mobile. As he travels, Jim will continue to create and ideate. He'll continue to help others to tell the stories of their search for God.

A future built of blogs

To understand the recent evolution of the artistic process, it is helpful to understand the mechanisms by which art can be shared in virtual contexts. Blogging is one of these mechanisms. Derived from "web" and "log," a blog is simply a digital diary, and blogging is digital self-publishing. Bloggers have wide latitude in what they create and share. They can write anything from recipes, parenting tips, theological reflections, sports rants, or political commentary. Their only requirement is that they must post it to a site that easily accommodates new content, while providing easy access to existing content.

The *Blog Tyrant Blog*, a blog about blogs, asked 350 bloggers about their interest in this digital form of self-publishing. They found that nearly half of those surveyed spend five hours or fewer per week on their blog, and nearly two-thirds of bloggers have never made any money from their content.[6] While blogs can be professional, forty-hours-per-week endeavors, most are simply thoughtful side-hustles. Between three hundred million and one billion in number, they are expressions of the artistic process. They are an attempt to share their perspectives with those who will listen. They are a digital canvas for the internet age, a simple block of marble that can be sculpted into anything that our minds might dream up.

The digital age has seen explosive growth in blogging. Google acquired Blogger in 2003. Sensing the imminent growth of digital self-expression, and seeing the monetization opportunities from advertising on these platforms, Google purchased the four-year-old web logging startup for an undisclosed amount.[7] By providing free hosting, storage, and site templates to anyone with a Google account, Google expanded user access to an ever-increasing number of web artists. As of 2019, Blogger was the second-most widely used blogging platform, just behind WordPress (although WordPress is much more widely used for the design and publication of business websites, which likely overstates its usage metrics).[8] Google's blogging platform is among the most user-friendly blogging platforms. I have used it for blogs about my travels, my career, and theology.

I mention blogs because they represent a low-tech way to create, curate, and share stories in a faith community. The church of tech-shaped culture will engage blogs as platforms where faith communities coalesce around a topic. Church leaders of the digital age will curate blogs that provide a space for individuals to articulate and share their experience with God. Our ability to bring the Gospel message to a tech-shaped culture will depend on our willingness to identify the faith stories around us, and to ensure those stories are told.

Quiz: Is your congregation a storytelling congregation?

Respond to the following questions to identify how your faith community could more consistently embrace creativity through storytelling.

1. Every sermon preached in our congregation includes a personal story, anecdote, or experience.　　　　　　　　　　Yes ○ No ○
2. In the past twelve months, at least one non-staff lay member from the congregation has preached a sermon.　　　　　　Yes ○ No ○

3. In the past twelve months, a sermon took
   the form of an "interview" between a pastor
   (the interviewer) and a community member
   (the storyteller).   Yes ○ No ○
4. Faith formation events, perhaps including
   Sunday school, confirmation, and adult
   education, provide consistent opportunities for
   learners to articulate their faith experience.   Yes ○ No ○
5. The congregation uses digital media (podcasts,
   videos, social media, and the like) to enable
   from members of our community to tell
   their personal faith stories.   Yes ○ No ○

For reflection and discussion

1. Faith communities embrace many different kinds of stories, including narratives about where one has seen God at work and how one sees God at work in their vocation. Which type of story would resonate most with your faith community?
2. Digital media platforms, including YouTube, Facebook, and Twitter, create easy opportunities to create and share stories. Which platform do you have the most experience with, and how could you use that platform to help the community share their faith stories?

Creativity: ideas for worship	
High-tech	Fill the sanctuary with digital visual arts created by the community. Invite the community to create photos, graphics, or collages in response to a liturgical season or preaching theme. Display their work using projectors and screens.
Low-tech	Use projector screens to display song lyrics, photographs, and paintings that align to the music and readings. Encourage community members to contribute to these slide shows using free apps like Prezi or Animoto.
No-tech	Expand the number of stories told from the pulpit. Invite lay church members to provide sermons on a regular basis.

13

Reimaging Church with Creative Messiness

The creative process and the world of technology share in common a certain level of comfort with messiness, ambiguity, and failure. If church leaders in a tech-shaped culture are to embrace creativity, they ought to simultaneously develop a certain level of comfort with trying new approaches, a capacity to move beyond the many approaches that flop, and a resiliency to try new creative endeavors in the face of adversity.

One of my most direct encounters with the collision of creativity and failure happened while I was working at Google. "Come to the office town hall to learn about the company's big bet on social," read the email from our office's new Google+ "solutions" team. It was July 2011 and I had barely been a Googler for one month. Already, the company was undergoing transformational change. Larry Page, the C.E.O., had demanded that all employees find a way to support the success of a project code-named "Emerald Sea."

The "Emerald Sea" project started with creative origins and plenty of momentum. Every employee in the company was given a limited number of exclusive access codes to Google+, the company's first attempt at a feed-based social network. When the news got out that I could get my friends into this elite online club, my phone began to buzz incessantly. College roommates, high school classmates, former football teammates—they all wanted in on this new social media phenomenon.

Google+ began as a feed-based social network, similar to Facebook or Twitter. It offered three innovations, though, that those other social networks had not yet thought of. First, Google+ empowered users to share posts only with certain "circles." You could share photos from your college graduation with your family circle, photos of your post-graduation bar crawl with your friends circle, and pleas for assistance in finding a job in your professionals circle. In a time where all social media content was automatically broadcast to every social media connection, Google+ provided precision, and by extension, a bit of privacy. Second, Google+ included a native video messaging application: Google Hangouts. With Hangouts, you could call anyone in your circles with audio and video. Hangouts were faster and more reliable than other video conference competitors. It was also free to users with a Google+ profile. Finally, Google+ offered vastly improved photo storage. In a time where Facebook photos were grainy, blurry, and effectively useless if downloaded, Google+ offered high resolution and markedly improved quality. It's no surprise that photographers were among the earliest adopters of the new social network.

Google swiftly activated its vast employee base to evangelize what became known internally as "G plus." Sales teams were rewarded when their clients launched Google+ profile pages. Engineers ensured that activity on company Google+ pages appeared on advertisements throughout the web. Customer service representatives helped businesses to curate and respond to reviews on the platform. Soon, Google+ was marketed both as a social network and as a platform for businesses to strengthen ties with their customers.

With improved technology for social sharing, and a precise focus on driving business adoption, Google+ raced to a meteoric start. Employees received internal emails heralding the network as the "fastest growing" social platform of all time. When I saw several friends posting "I've left Facebook—and moved to Google+," I solidified my assumption that the latest Google venture would be an unquestioned success, another accomplishment in a prolific lineage that included Search, Gmail, and YouTube.

When I left Google in 2016, internal communications about Google+ had all but ceased. It had long been evident that the product had flopped. Sales teams were no longer extolling its ability to build meaningful connections between businesses and consumers. Senior leaders mentioned the platform with decreasing frequency in company-wide meetings. Managers stopped encouraging their direct reports to use the network for professional purposes. As I was concluding my time at the company, employees no longer saw Google+ as the "social future" of the internet.

In December of 2018, Google began to shut down Google+.[1] While there are many theories explaining its collapse, I attribute its expensive demise mostly to poor timing. Launched in the same year as Snapchat, Google+ had to overcome an intense migration of social activity *away* from feed-based tools like Facebook *towards* private messaging applications. The momentum of messaging tools proved to be too much for a feed-based platform to overcome.

Yet it was not a total loss. Google+ surely influenced other social networks, Facebook included, to provide greater control over where content was shared. Google+ also provided the infrastructure for Google Photos, a widely used photo storage and sharing application that offers even higher image quality than its predecessor. I maintain that Google+ came from a highly creative idea and evolved into an innovative product, launched at exactly the wrong moment. Launched even two to three years earlier, Google+ may well have been a success.

Sometimes, creative efforts fail, not because of a lack of effort, expertise, or investment, but because of circumstances far beyond our individual control. From the rise and fall of Google+, we can learn important lessons for church leadership in a tech-shaped culture.

Empty social networks and empty churches

When I worked as a ministry intern, my church had dozens of active and engaged students in the youth group. Part of my job as a ministry intern was to keep the momentum going throughout the summer, to build and lead a weekly Bible study, and to continue building spiritual community outside of the academic year. I quickly came up with two ideas. First, we would have a weekly Bible study with a baseball theme. Not everyone was enthusiastic about studying the scriptures on a beautiful summer evening, but who didn't love America's pastime?

I spent nearly one month preparing for this baseball-themed Bible study. Each week, we would look at a different "lesson" learned through the game of baseball: perseverance, commitment, service. We would then study and discuss a Bible passage related to that lesson. The evening would conclude with some baseball watching, either the Milwaukee Brewers on television, or their local minor-league affiliate, the Wisconsin Timber Rattlers, whose games were played just down the road for an affordable price of admission.

I created a brochure about the Bible study, posted it to the church website and bulletin board, and sent emails to youth and parents alike. "Baseball and Bibles" would be the spiritual innovation of the summer of 2008, a near-certain tactic for strengthening faith and keeping the community strong through the summer months.

That first night, I arrived at church early. I arranged the comfortable chairs, set up the television, and arranged the snacks. I even set up a Bible-themed baseball board game that I had found earlier that day at the thrift shop! I donned my Brewers ball cap and took a seat, waiting for the group to arrive.

But nobody did. I waited and waited, thinking the youth were just running late. And then the Brewers game started. I watched the first pitch, then the first inning. The next thing I knew, it was the bottom of the fourth, the Brewers were losing, and I was sitting in an empty church by myself. "Baseball and Bibles" had flopped, and it would continue to flop, for four weeks, until we decided to discontinue the program.

As it turns out, a weekday evening is a particularly poor scheduling choice for high school youth during the summertime. Many are working in an attempt to save money for a car payment or college tuition. Others are at baseball or basketball practice. Some are simply enjoying the summer sun, reluctant to commit to several hours in a dimly lit church. Like Google+, the timing was all wrong. The ideas were creative, the program well-envisioned, yet it flopped.

What worked well that summer wasn't the intensively-planned "Baseball and Bibles." It was a weekly lunch at the Buffalo Wild Wings, adjacent from the Fox River Mall. Every Thursday, I invited the high schoolers in the church to gather for fifty cent boneless chicken wings and conversation. Many kids would attend. The Buffalo Wild Wings staff came to know us on a first-name basis. The kids received the affirming presence of a faith community invested in hearing about the ups and downs of their summer. I received weekly heartburn. I also learned the importance of community in faith development. Even though that community gathered around boneless wings instead of Bibles, it still fostered connection and collaboration. It still allowed for questions. That's what that summer was about. Over Dr. Peppers and Blazin' BBQ, the kids shared their stories, asked questions about God, and experienced the power of Christian community. It helped that most of those kids worked at the mall—near Buffalo Wild Wings, making it a far easier commitment than my baseball idea. For one hour and nine dollars every week, we were fed with fried and heavenly food—strength for our spiritual searches.

S'More Camp

Technological innovation flops in the church as often as it does anywhere. I spent my college summers working as a summer camp counselor at Pine Lake Camp, a Lutheran camping ministry in Waupaca, Wisconsin. Pine Lake is one of three camps serving the Lutheran churches of Northeast Wisconsin and is often brimming with energetic, hormonal adolescents. In 2009 and 2010, most of our campers didn't have a smartphone to surrender, which meant a solid week away from Facebook. Back then, Facebook had achieved peak popularity among middle and high school aged youth. This was prior to Snapchat, prior to Instagram stories, but after the now archaic AOL Instant Messenger.

As a camp staff, we didn't know what to do with Facebook. Our campers all had profiles on Facebook. So did our camp staff. It was inevitable that these young, impressionable youth would find camp counselors, who they held in such high esteem, and connect with them on the social network. This set off many boundary alarms within the camp leadership. What would happen if a counselor was photographed at a college party? What would happen if a camper viewed those photos? Would it wreck the image the camper had of their Christian role model?

These were important concerns. Boundaries matter in the world of church, and they matter when spirituality goes online. Throughout staff training, counselors were continuously reminded that they were not to engage with any campers on Facebook. They were not to add campers as friends. They were not to send any messages to campers. It was actually just those two rules, which somehow necessitated approximately eight hours' worth of training time, some of it with the camp director, some with the executive director, and some with the bishop of the synod. I suppose their aversion adequately illustrated the church's initial hesitancy to integrate ministry with new technologies.

Fortunately, there was a Facebook alternative, safe, secure, and devoid of unsavory social media content (though to be truthful, it was devoid of any content). The camp devised a solution that campers could connect with their camp counselors on the S'More Camp social network, where they could swap pictures of camp and reminisce about the great times and the tick bites alike. That summer, every camper left with detailed information on setting up a S'More Camp profile and connecting with the Pine Lake Camp community.

S'More Camp was to Facebook what the Mini Disc was to CD-Rom, or what Microsoft Zune was to Apple iPod. Without a critical mass of participants, without photos, stories, and groups, without any of the messages and reactions and gimmicks that make Facebook so addicting, S'More Camp was destined to be about as beloved as poison ivy. But we tried our best. We mentioned S'More Camp in skits. Some of us provided campers with our S'More Camp contact information. To my knowledge, none of us on staff had posted anything to S'More Camp by the end of the summer, and none of the campers had bothered to set up a profile page.

I'm an advocate of camping ministry, but I'm still not a S'More Camp user. While it was designed to address a valid concern about the confluence of faith, technology, and boundaries, its design was unoriginal and its value proposition unclear. Still, I don't fault the camp staff or S'More Camp for this ultimately unsuccessful effort. It was an attempt at establishing connections between searchers in a digital age, valiant effort met with an underwhelming payoff. It's precisely these unsuccessful ventures that can point the church of a tech-shaped culture in the direction of innovation. We need more flops like S'More Camp. We need more thoughtful risk taking. Sometimes, our shared search for God moves forward not through success, but by the simple act of trying.

Failing fast

"We in the church have a challenge with failing fast or failing in public," says Keith Anderson. "I certainly have found that even in the mistakes I have made—something in that work was so good or innovative. I'm going to come back to it and pull that out later on. I'm going to learn from it, and I'm going to use it."

Anderson notes that despite the necessity of learning through experimentation and failure in a digital age, religion has never tolerated failure well. "As a pastor, I'm supposed to preach my polished, complete, finished sermon. It's supposed to be perfect. We're trained in the church to have everything appear polished, and this needs to change. It's a real growing edge to let go not just of our perfectionism, but of our need for control."

For Pastor Keith, failing fast means letting go of the need to always have the right answer. He recently started a Theology on Tap meetup in the Philadelphia area.

> I regularly gather at a local tavern for about 75 minutes of discussion on a given topic. Theology on Tap is a faith formation forum for adults, many of whom wouldn't come to church. We meet to discuss a specific topic—the holy spirit, the afterlife, it can be anything. The evening is full of questions—but rarely does it end with a single, concise answer. Church has this need to supply all the answers. That doesn't work today. Part of failing fast is to accept incomplete conclusions and unanswered questions.

As Anderson wrote in a recent blog post, "The value of the church's presence in digital and local gathering spaces is not to find conversations about Christianity and co-opt them, but to listen and nurture relationship and conversation with those that are moving faith forward, who are reshaping Christianity apart from the institutional church."[2]

It is critical that the Christian tradition, long known for its pomp and polish, develop a comfort with what always accompanies creativity: trial and error, and inevitable failure. In the digital age, trial, error, and failure are indicators of innovation, markers of full participation in the creative process.

For reflection and discussion

- To what extent are failure and creativity related? Do you see failure as an occasional and inevitable result of innovation?
- Have you attempted to launch or implement something innovative at your church, only to see it flop or fall apart? If so, why do you think the effort was unsuccessful?
- What did you learn from the experience that could influence future attempts at innovation?
- Why, in a time of dwindling church attendance, is it important for church leaders to develop a certain comfort with failure?

Creativity: ideas for faith formation and Christian education	
High-tech	Center a class around creating a church podcast. Meet up to introduce a theme for the course. Provide space and equipment for learners to record a short story in response to the theme. Edit and publish the podcast as a class.
Low-tech	Invite learners to reflect on their learning using Instagram Stories. Give them space to take, edit, and annotate photographs in response to a reading or discussion, and curate their posts on the church Instagram page.
No-tech	Have the instructor set an example of using personal narratives in Christian education. When presenting any contextual information, always provide a personal story demonstrating why these topics matter to your faith life.

Conclusion:
Being Church in
a Tech-Shaped Culture

I wrote this book, in part, to explore the intersection of two seemingly different worlds in which I have spent considerable time: the world of church, and the world of digital technology. As I reflected on the world of digital technology, it didn't take long to recognize that all of us in this tech-shaped culture share certain values, the values of questions, connections, collaboration, and creativity. As I reflected on the world of church, it didn't take too much effort to realize that many of our ways of being the church are disconnected from these values.

Throughout this book, I have argued that the challenge of church in a culture gone digital is primarily about alignment. Digital technology is changing how culture thinks, learns, and believes, and church needs to adapt. This transformation can and will not happen by improving our usage of technology, bettering our marketing, or improving the polish with which we tell God's story. Rather, this transformation will happen when we engage the values of a digital age, which includes making space for questions, finding new ways of connection, facilitating collaboration, and promoting creativity.

I am optimistic about the future of church. The Christian tradition has been here before, situated in a time of great technological and cultural change, confronted with the challenge of finding new ways of proclaiming the Gospel to a world that needs to hear it. And when the church has faced similar challenges in the past, innovative leaders have discovered new ways of telling the Good News.

As I think about all the new technology around us, I can't help but think of Johannes Gutenberg's printing press and the influence it had on Christianity. Gutenberg finished a commercially viable version of his machine of mass textual production in 1450. Likely similar machines existed in India and China several hundred years before his version, but Gutenberg's was the first printing press in western Europe. The European device, built upon the innovation of movable type, facilitated the rapid transmission of the written word (by sixteenth-century standards). Gutenberg's press meant that copying was no longer the work of a professional and highly skilled class of scribes tethered to monastic writing tables for hours on end. Any educated European with access to Gutenberg's could send their word to the masses. Even more significantly, they could get their word out without the editing, approval, and censorship of church and civil authorities.

The invention of the printing press catalyzed a seismic change in western culture, which became increasingly literate, educated, and, for better or worse, individualistic. At the beginning of the sixteenth century, the European literacy rate was approximately ten percent. By 1600, that rate had climbed to fifty percent.[1] One hundred fifty years after Gutenberg's invention, half of Europe's population could read a text and react to it independently, applying their own judgments to written work that was previously accessible and understandable exclusively to cultural elites. In the centuries to come, European spirituality would become more didactic and more concerned with the individual's interpretation and understanding of the scriptures.

Gutenberg's technological revolution catalyzed the Protestant Reformation, creating a paradigm shift in what it means to be the church.

The Reformation was born not just out of Luther's theological brilliance but out of his savvy awareness of how the printing press was transforming culture. He translated the Bible into the vernacular and championed the idea that God saves by grace through faith. But Luther's ideas would have been confined to the cloister were it not for his ability to respond to his cultural moment. Luther was certainly a skilled technologist, but his greatest aptitude was his awareness of a culture that was becoming more literate, more learned, and more autonomous. As Luther's printed work spread across Christendom, his readers began thinking differently about their Christian expression. Luther and his contemporaries began calling into question the necessity of former ways of doing church, challenging traditional structures, and testing radical new concepts.

The history of the Christian witness is a story of leaders who continuously reformed and transformed in response to changes in culture that were often catalyzed by technology. Ultimately, church thrived through these cultural and technological changes because it aligned to a new cultural landscape. In these previous technological revolutions, those stewarding the tradition fundamentally changed the way they told the "old, old story."

While the church benefited greatly through its mastery of the movable-type printing press, that does not suggest, as I've said before, that being church in a digital age is about using or succeeding with a particular technology or achieving success on a particular platform. Ultimately, using new technology and adapting to the culture that arises from it is about understanding our neighbor—who they are, what they value, and how they construct meaning. In our era, it's about making space for our neighbor's questions, creating connections in hybrid contexts, establishing a collaborative environment, and embracing innovation and messiness.

There are many possible first steps towards becoming the church of the digital age and reaching those who are searching for God with

Google, and we might feel overwhelmed when we consider how to proceed. My recommendation: Choose small steps that will bring your mission, the Gospel message, and the values of a tech-shaped culture into alignment. When it seems that something is clearly not working, try something else. But don't try too hard. The blessings of the digital age include questions, connection, collaboration, and creativity. The curse of the digital age is multitasking and an addiction to taking too much on at once. Whatever type of faith community you lead, whether you are a lay person or a pastor, a community member or a bishop, the future of the Christian witness depends upon our willingness to innovate, one creative endeavor at a time.

Searching for a future that is God's

It was raining the day I graduated from Luther Seminary. Not the type of warm, gentle rain you expect on a late May afternoon. It was a windy deluge that ruptured umbrellas and contorted faces of those who entered Central Lutheran Church in Minneapolis for Luther's 150th commencement. As I sat in the pews of the great downtown church and watched my classmates walk to receive their diplomas, I was occupied by thoughts of the coming work week. The late afternoon commencement would be followed by a long night of driving, which would lead to a short night of sleep and a restless start to the week ahead.

There were many conversations about the future during that final weekend at Luther Seminary, and as faculty and student speakers delivered the charge to bring love and justice into the world, I realized I was somewhat alone. Surrounded by over one-hundred fellow graduates, I was acutely aware that our long-shared paths were about to diverge. The friends I had studied with for over four years would soon take a bold new step in their career, most soon beginning their first calls as pastors.

Many would be the only pastor in their new vocational homes. Some would be the only staff member.

I would be returning to the Zendesk office the next morning for another week of my career in the technology industry—to the same job, the same career path, the same open office surroundings I had left the previous Friday evening. The dean read my name. I stepped onto the makeshift stage to receive my diploma and to be hooded with the insignia befitting the degree. I was filled with pride—and just a hint of isolation. A master's degree in theology and a job in the technology industry is not a conventional vocational path. But as far as I can tell from years of study, work, and professional discernment, it is the unique path to which God has called me.

Ever since I began my career at Google, those in the church world have asked me for advice on technology. I've helped pastors to launch websites, I've encouraged youth ministers to start an Instagram feed, and I've fixed misconfigured audio-visual equipment far too many times. I've helped churches share files on Google Drive. I've helped Lutheran camps start advertising with Google AdWords and measure the quality of site traffic with Google Analytics. I've helped them to use Facebook to raise funds on "Giving Tuesday." Listed in one document, these previous years would overfill a resume with tasks completed at the intersection of church and tech—with tactics adopted at the merging of ministry and the internet.

Part of what led me to write this book was the realization that all of these efforts have been at the same time personally fulfilling and deeply frustrating. Despite my best efforts, the church will never have the best websites, the freshest feeds, or the savviest marketing campaigns. We'll never be completely up to date on website design trends. We'll always be a step behind the rest of the world when it comes to technological adoption. And even if we in the church did manage these things, it wouldn't be enough to halt the accelerating decline of institutional

Christianity; the cultural headwinds are far too strong. Interest in spirituality in America may be alive and well, but pews and coffers are emptying faster than we would like to admit. Church cannot "compete" with high-tech organizations in the digital age.

And that is the beautiful, paradoxical good news. Because the story of faith gone online is not the story of tactical excellence, technological innovation, or digital expertise. It's not a story of tools, and it never will be. The story of faith gone digital is the story of a revolution that has steadily altered the way we think, the way we believe, and what we choose to value. It's the story of how ubiquitous platforms like Google and Apple, Facebook and Snapchat, Twitter and YouTube have changed the way we think, learn, and know. The successful technology platforms in the digital age are successful because they call us to question and help us to connect. These platforms reach wide audiences because they facilitate collaboration; they celebrate and socialize creativity. Whether we look at Google or Microsoft, Uber or LinkedIn, or the myriad other technologies that give shape to our contemporary experience, we see the commonalities of questions, connection, collaboration, and creativity. Ultimately, these technologies are not giving us tools—they're instilling within us a mindset.

So many of us in the church want to do ministry with, for, and alongside those in a tech-shaped culture. I hope that this book has helped church leaders to recognize that what matters in this tech-shaped culture is not the quality of our technology but whether our practices align to a changed cultural mindset.

I didn't linger much after the commencement ceremony concluded. I had a long drive ahead of me, an early morning meeting to begin the work week, and several looming deadlines to confront. I joked with my wife that the lukewarm Lime Lacroix in the cup holder would have to substitute for a bottle of champagne. We merged onto I-94 in a rain splattered acceleration, dodging potholes while activating the windshield wipers. Construction barrels loomed in the distance as the spires of Central Lutheran faded from view. That fleeting weekend pause for celebration had ended. The time for building something new was just ahead on the horizon.

Notes

Introduction

1. *Merriam-Webster Online*, "Google." accessed July 1, 2019. https://www.merriam-webster.com/dictionary/google.
2. Laura Stampler, "Amazon Just Became the Most Valuable Public Company in the U.S." *Fortune*, January 7, 2019, https://tinyurl.com/svtma6x.
3. Mary Hess (Professor of Educational Leadership at Luther Seminary), in discussion with the author, August 2019.
4. Michael Lipka, "Millennials Increasingly Are Driving Growth of 'Nones'." Pew Research Center, May 12, 2015, https://tinyurl.com/smj2sj8.
5. Lipka, "Millennials."
6. Dwight Zscheile, "Will the ELCA Be Gone in 30 Years?" *Faith + Lead*, September 5, 2019, accessed November 14, 2019, https://faithlead.luthersem.edu/decline/.
7. Allison Pond, Gregory Smith, and Scott Clement. "Religion Among the Millennials." Pew Research Center, February 17, 2010. https://tinyurl.com/tjvw6tc

Chapter 1: Asking Our Own Questions

1. "Who Is Jesus?" Google Trends, accessed July 1, 2019. https://tinyurl.com/rlfobee..
2. Google does not release raw statistics on search volume, though their Google Trends tool presents normalized ranges for the sake of comparison, as seen in the threefold increase in the search "Who is Jesus" from Christmas 2007 to Christmas 2017.

Chapter 2: The Past: A Church that Silences Questions

1. Eric Schmidt, Jonathan Rosenberg, and Alan Eagle. *How Google Works* (New York: Grand Central Publishing, 2017), 107. According to dictionary.com,

myopia is a synonym for nearsightedness—in this case, involving a lack of creativity, imagination, or insight.

2. Parker J. Palmer. *The Courage to Teach: Exploring the Inner Landscape of a Teachers Life* (Hoboken, NJ: Jossey-Bass, 2017).

Chapter 3: The Future: A Church that Celebrates Questions

1. Stephanie Williams O'Brien (author of *Stay Curious*), in conversation with the author, December 2019.

Section 2: Connection

1. Claire Groden, "71% Of Smartphone Owners Sleep with Them." *Fortune*, June 29, 2015. https://tinyurl.com/uqc224z.
2. Clive Thompson, "Are You Checking Work Email in Bed? At the Dinner Table? On Vacation?" *Mother Jones*, June 2014, https://tinyurl.com/vno9h9d.
3. "History of Gmail." *Wikipedia*, last modified, November 20, 2019, 23:45 https://en.wikipedia.org/wiki/History_of_Gmail.
4. Taylor Kerns, "Gmail Now Has More than 1.5 Billion Active Users," *Android Police*, October 26, 2018, https://tinyurl.com/yc2haa26.
5. Steven Levy, *In the Plex: How Google Thinks, Works, and Shapes Our Lives* (New York: Simon & Schuster, 2011), 169.

Chapter 4: Finding New Ways to Connect

1. Sarah Stonesifer Boylan (Digital Missioner for Lifelong Learning at Virginia Theological Seminary), in discussion with the author, June 2019.
2. Heidi Campbell (Professor of Communications at Texas A&M University), in discussion with the author, June 2019.
3. Robert Putnam, *Bowling Alone: The Collapse and Revival of American Community* (New York: Simon & Schuster, 2000), 66.
4. "Attendance at Religious Services: Religious Landscapes Study," Pew Research Center, Washington, D.C. (May 11, 2015) https://tinyurl.com/vfg5vyr.
5. Carol Tucker, "The 1950s–Powerful Years for Religion." *USC News*, June 16, 1997, https://tinyurl.com/ya8rew2m.
6. Pew Research Center, "Attendance at Religious Services."

Chapter 5: Redefining Offline Connection

1. Libby Seline, "Pastor's 'Rant' initiates honest conversations about religion with students," *The Daily Nebraskan*, Feb. 3, 2019, https://tinyurl.com/w6us4hp.
2. Adam White (Campus pastor at the University of Nebraska-Lincoln), in discussion with the author, May 2019.

3. "Madison Neighborhood Indicators Project," Madison, Wisconsin, accessed June 1, 2019. https://madison.apl.wisc.edu/.
4. Joe Brosius (Pastor, Good Shepherd Lutheran Church), in discussion with the author, May 2019.

Chapter 6: Integrating Online Connection

1. DJ Soto (Pastor and author of *Click2Save*), in discussion with the author, May 2019.
2. Heidi Campbell and Louise Connelly, "Religion in a Networked Society," June 10, 2013, in Religious Studies Project, podcast, https://tinyurl.com /r23rrkk.
3. "Experiences," VR Church, accessed August 1, 2019, https://www.vrchurch .org/experiences.
4. Paul Lamkin, "VR And AR Headsets to Hit 80 Million By 2021." *Forbes*, September 29, 2017. https://tinyurl.com/smmz6jr.
5. VR Church, "Experiences."
6. DJ Soto, discussion.
7. Bryce Covert, "Americans Work Too Much Already." *The Nation*, September 28, 2018. https://tinyurl.com/rgdzcv9.
8. Lydia Saad, "The '40-Hour' Workweek Is Actually Longer—by Seven Hours." *Gallup*, May 16, 2019, https://tinyurl.com/y8dffuaw.
9. "American Community Survey Data." The United States Census Bureau accessed September 26, 2019. https://tinyurl.com/r2y2lkl.
10. "Safety and Health at the Heart of the Future of Work: Building on 100 Years of Experience," International Labour Organization, accessed, April 18, 2019. https://tinyurl.com/wgm78n2.
11. Adam Schuele, "Sabbath," in *New Interpreter's Dictionary of the Bible*." (Nashville: Abingdon Press, August 2009) 3.
12. Christin Tomy. "Sabbath as a Radical Act," in *National Catholic Reporter* 54, no. 6, 2017, 1a–4a.
13. Adam Schuele, "Sabbath," in *New Interpreter's Dictionary of the Bible*." (Nashville: Abingdon Press, August 2009) 6.
14. Jim Boyce (Professor Emeritus of New Testament at Luther Seminary), in discussion with the author, June 2019.

Chapter 7: Connecting with the Whole Person

1. Heidi Campbell (Professor of Communications at Texas A&M University), in discussion with the author, June 2019.
2. Shamika Goddard (PhD student, University of Colorado), in discussion with the author, June 2019
3. Shamika Goddard, "What Is a Tech Chaplain?" *Techchaplaincy.com*, accessed August 1, 2019. https://tinyurl.com/tp9ooc3.

Notes

Chapter 8: Learning and Leading Collaboratively

1. Paresh Dave, "Google's G Suite Is No Microsoft Killer, but Still Winning Converts." *Reuters*, February 1, 2018. https://tinyurl.com/y8snauc8.
2. Frederic Lardinois, "Google Updates Drive with a Focus on Its Business Users." *TechCrunch*, March 9, 2017. https://tinyurl.com/s7t72kh.

Chapter 9: Learning and Faith Formation

1. Palmer. *The Courage to Teach"* p. 52.
2. Palmer. *The Courage to Teach*, p. 54.
3. Lubos Janoska, "What Really Is the Cone Of Experience?" *eLearning Industry*, August 28, 2017. https://tinyurl.com/t8u7lmp

Chapter 10: Collaboration and Shared Leadership

1. Virginia Theological Seminary, "EFormation Learning Community Home," accessed July 1, 2019. https://eformationvts.org/.
2. Sarah Stonesifer (Digital Missioner for Lifelong Learning at Virginia Theological Seminary), in discussion with the author, June 2019.
3. Stonesifer, discussion
4. The Joshua Group, "Fulfilling Purpose," accessed August 1, 2019. https://thejoshua-group.com/.
5. Kristin Wiersma (Consultant, The Joshua Group), in conversation with the author, May 2019.
6. Wiersma, discussion.
7. Wiersma, discussion.
8. Wiersma, discussion.
9. David Kelley, "Design Thinking," *IDEO*, accessed August 16, 2019. https://www.ideou.com/pages/design-thinking.

Section 4: Creativity

1. Steven Levy, *In the Plex: How Google Thinks, Works, and Shapes Our Lives* (New York: Simon & Schuster, 2011), 249.
2. Jillian D'Onfro, "YouTube Still Doesn't Make Google Any Money." Business Insider, February 25, 2015. https://tinyurl.com/uh2rrqt.
3. Effective YouTube Advertising Strategy," *Google*, accessed July 1, 2019. https://tinyurl.com/sbknll2.
4. Dave Davies, "The 7 Most Popular Search Engines in the World," *Search Engine Journal*, January 7, 2018. https://tinyurl.com/rwq2cbg.
5. Darrell Etherington, "People Now Watch 1 Billion Hours of YouTube per Day," *TechCrunch*, February 28, 2017. https://tinyurl.com/y8ch2l3g.

6. "Top Four Content Categories on YouTube." *Google,* accessed August 1, 2019. https://tinyurl.com/vxjx633.

Chapter 11: Encountering Christ through Creating

1. Richard Rohr, "Art: Week 1 Summary," Center for Action and Contemplation, May 19, 2018. https://tinyurl.com/rbvcy9j.
2. Martin Luther, *Luther's Works, Volume 40: Church and Ministry II*, ed. Conrad Bergendoff and Helmut H. Lehman, (Minneapolis, Minnesota: Fortress Press, 1958), 99.
3. Michael Gungor, "The Problem With Christian Art," *Relevant Magazine*, February 15, 2013. https://tinyurl.com/v785z4l.

Chapter 12: Creating Faith through Story

1. Dave Daubert (author, pastor, and consultant), in conversation with the author, June 2019.
2. Anderson, conversation.
3. Darleen Pryds (Associate Professor of Christian Spirituality and History, Franciscan School of Theology), in conversation with the author, May 2019.
4. "Darleen Pryds, PhD." Franciscan School of Theology, accessed September 1, 2019. https://tinyurl.com/srrjkmf.
5. Jim Keat (Associate Minister of Digital Strategy and Online Engagement at The Riverside Church in New York City), in conversation with the author, May 2014.
6. "The Latest Blogging Trends and Statistics for 2020 (and Beyond)." *Blog Tyrant*, January 14, 2020. https://www.blogtyrant.com/new-blogging-statistics/.
7. Levy, *In the Plex*, 101.
8. "Blog Usage Distribution in the United States," *Built With*, Accessed September 1, 2019. https://tinyurl.com/tdamzmc.

Chapter 13: Reimaging Church with Creative Messiness

1. "Shutting down Google for Consumer (Personal) Accounts on April 2, 2019," *Google*, January 30, 2019. https://tinyurl.com/tvv6d2e.
2. Keith Anderson, "Re-Mediation in the D-I-Y Church," *The BTS Center*, October 2017, https://tinyurl.com/vaj87lu.

Conclusion: Being Church in a Tech-Shaped Culture

1. William A Pelz, " 'The Other Reformation": Martin Luther, Religious Dogma and the Common People," *A People's History of Modern Europe*, (London: Pluto Press, 2016), 18–29, doi:10.2307/j.ctt1c2crfj.6.